PEACEBUILDING THROUGH COMMUNITY-BASED NGOS

16347148 45.00

PEACEBUILDING THROUGH COMMUNITY-BASED NGOs
PARADOXES AND POSSIBILITIES

MAX STEPHENSON JR. AND LAURA ZANOTTI

Kumarian Press
An Imprint of Stylus Publishing
Sterling, Virginia

Published by Stylus Publishing, LLC
22883 Quicksilver Drive
Sterling, Virginia 20166-2102

Design by Pro Production Graphic Services
Copyedit by Bob Land
Proofread by Beth Richards
Index by Manjit Sahai
The text of this book is set in 11/13 Adobe Garamond

Printed in the United States of America

∞ All first editions printed on acid-free paper that meets the American National Standards Institute Z39-48 Standard.

Library of Congress Cataloging-in-Publication Data
Stephenson, Max O.
  Peacebuilding through community-based NGOs : paradoxes and possibilities /
Max Stephenson, Jr. and Laura Zanotti. — 1st ed.
      p. cm.
  Includes bibliographical references and index.
  ISBN 978-1-56549-427-5 (cloth : alk. paper) — ISBN 978-1-56549-426-8
(pbk. : alk. paper) — ISBN 978-1-56549-428-2 (library networkable e-edition) —
ISBN 978-1-56549-429-9 (consumer e-edition)
  1. Peace-building—Social aspects. 2. Non-governmental organizations. 3. Peace-building—
Social aspects—Case studies. 4. Non-governmental organizations—Case studies. I. Zanotti,
Laura. II. Title.
  JZ5538.S7425 2012
  303.6'6—dc23

                                                                      2012006920

13-digit ISBN: 978-1-56549-427-5 (cloth)
13-digit ISBN: 978-1-56549-426-8 (paper)
13-digit ISBN: 978-1-56549-428-2 (library networkable e-edition)
13-digit ISBN: 978-1-56549-429-9 (consumer e-edition)

Bulk Purchases

Quantity discounts are available for use in workshops and for staff development.

Call 1-800-232-0223

First Edition, 2012

    10 9 8 7 6 5 4 3 2 1

For Jessica:
You are daily an example of hope and courage. MOS

For Giovanni:
Keep questioning what you are told. LZ

Contents

Acknowledgments

This book is the result of a collaboration of two scholars with different theoretical orientations and backgrounds, but with a shared interest in exploring the outcomes and effects of nongovernmental organizations (NGOs) as increasingly important stakeholders in post-conflict peacebuilding initiatives worldwide. Max Stephenson Jr. is interested in collaborative governance structures and processes, social imaginaries, and the possibilities for reconciliation and change in post-conflict societies. Laura Zanotti's research focuses on international intervention, critical political theory, and the possibility of political agency in blurring spaces of governance. Our aim is to provide a broad audience of readers with a contextual analysis of the impacts of the peace and human security efforts of different types of NGOs operating with different goals in very diverse post-conflict societies. We hope our analysis prompts reflection on the complexities facing nongovernmental organizations and international donors as they engage in post-conflict situations. We caution strongly against one-size-fits-all approaches to peacebuilding.

We are grateful to a number of institutions and colleagues for support of our efforts to complete this book. We wish to thank the Jerome Niles fund of the Virginia Tech College of Liberal Arts and Human Sciences for a generous research grant that supported a portion of our work, and the Virginia Tech Institute for Society, Culture and the Environment, which also generously enabled our research in Northern Ireland.

We wish, too, to acknowledge the support of three Virginia Tech Department of Political Science colleagues particularly, who offered insightful comments on our evolving effort: Professors Edward Weisband, Francois Debrix, and Jason Wiedner. Lyusyena Kirakosyan, a doctoral candidate in Virginia Tech's Alliance for Social, Political, Ethical and Cultural Thought program, also provided valuable observations. We thank them all. We are also indebted to the NGO professionals involved in the delicate and difficult business of (re)building societies and securing peace in post-conflict situations who gave so generously of their time to meet with us and to participate in interviews.

Finally, we would like to thank the officials of the United Nations Stabilization Mission in Haiti (MINUSTAH), who generously facilitated our fieldwork in that country. Some of those individuals perished in the 2010 Haiti earthquake, and we wish particularly to remember their kindness here.

We hope this volume honors the ongoing work of all those who are engaged in seeking to build peace in post-conflict societies and the memory of those who have lost their lives while engaged in such efforts. We are, of course, solely responsible for the views expressed here and for any errors of fact and interpretation that may remain.

1

NGOs, International Governance, and the Neoliberal Peacebuilding Consensus

Peace hath her Victories,
No less renown'd than war.
—John Milton

This book explores the contested but increasingly relevant role that non-governmental organizations (NGOs) are playing in promoting international peace, security, and development in the context of an emergent consensus around human security and neoliberal conceptualizations of good governance as organizing concepts for development initiatives. We argue that assessments of the role of NGOs as peacebuilders must be based on more than principled claims. Instead, they must be predicated on analyses of the complex, multi-actor contexts in which NGOs operate in post-conflict situations. Post-conflict societies are deeply politicized and, often, they are characterized by a multiplicity of actors seeking to build peace and bring about development. Each post-conflict nation exhibits distinctive economic, institutional, social, and administrative characteristics. Group and national identities in such countries are often rooted in the legacy of conflict that each has experienced. We are interested in whether, how, and in what circumstances international influence generally, and NGO engagement more specifically, may shape possibilities for social and political change. We assume that such efforts proceed today in the context of a prevailing international neoliberal definition of security, and the ongoing blurring among spaces and agents of governance that philosophical turn represents.

1

Accordingly, this book may be understood as an inquiry into the roles that NGO actors can play in eliciting or catalyzing possibilities for social and political change in post-conflict scenarios in the prevailing international context. While we are aware of the shortcomings of the neo-liberal consensus, which downplays the role of the state and delegates the realization of human security to the voluntary sector, we do not aim here to develop a critique of that ideology's road map for peace, or to propose a recipe for success in peacebuilding. Instead, we have sought to offer a contextualized assessment of how, under the existing international liberal peace consensus and given local conditions, the NGOs we considered contributed to broader goals of peacebuilding. We explore the successes as well as the shortcomings and occasional ironic effects of the efforts of the organizations we examined. As a result, this book raises questions concerning the homogenization and critical dismissals of NGOs as carriers of imperial agendas as well as romantic appraisals of their work as always benevolent or emancipating. While our goal was not to provide universal prescriptions of what good policy should look like, we nevertheless sought to explore several examples of attempted change in conflict scenarios and to examine the effects they have produced. We also articulate possibilities for engagement based on the strategies and outcomes of the actions of the NGOs we studied.

We analyze three NGOs that have played diverse roles in post-conflict situations: Partners In Health, Haiti, a health services and development organization; Women in Black–Serbia, a human rights advocacy organization; and the Community Foundation for Northern Ireland, a community-based philanthropy that has launched and sustained an array of grassroots-oriented peacebuilding efforts.

Our cases suggest that the effects of the international turn toward much-increased reliance on NGOs as instruments of peacebuilding and development have been mixed. We argue overall that the international community's choice to channel funds to NGOs as a primary instrument of peacebuilding and development in Haiti has had detrimental effects on state-building in that nation. Nevertheless, we also contend that some NGOs (our case example is Partners In Health) have created positive consequences for institution-building while also beneficially assisting the populations with which they work, which is a primary goal of international peacebuilding efforts. We also found that one advocacy NGO in the Balkans, whose efforts have focused on a narrow agenda of memorializing the victims of that region's conflict in the 1990s, has produced the unintended effect of hardening political identities and stifling reconciliation. In contrast, our research in Northern Ireland strongly suggested the utility of policymaker and intervener willingness to listen attentively to the groups in conflict and to seek to assist them in their long-term efforts to secure change by critically assessing narratives of conflict, rather than to aim to provide or impose a vision for peace or other superordinate aspiration for the conflicting parties.

We conclude not by offering yet another recipe for an imagined "best way" of bringing about peace through NGOs, but by highlighting some common characteristics of the organizations that have proven at least partially successful in achieving the results they set for themselves in the situations in which they operate. Our cases suggest that organizations that are locally rooted, maintain their financial independence, adopt a self-reflective approach, and remain engaged with the communities with which they work—rather than embracing preconceived prescriptions for bringing about peace—have performed better in achieving their goals and in limiting the unintended consequences of their presence and efforts.

Finally, a full-fledged discussion of the character and reach of civil society—including its relationship with states; its spontaneous or constructed nature; and an effort to delimit the differences, within the broad category of civil society institutions, between NGOs and grassroots or other organizations—is beyond the scope of this work. *Civil society* has been defined as occupying a space between the state and the market, but at the same time as possessing organizations that interact routinely with states (Chazan 1992). However, in post-conflict societies in particular, civil society must be viewed as the result of complex interactions between (competing) grassroots demands, state interests, and international strategies for peacebuilding and development.

In proposing criteria to distinguish between international NGOs and local grassroots ones, Marchetti and Tocci have argued, "The latter are often non voluntary in nature, less organized, less professional and have fewer human and financial resources at their disposal than their international counterparts" (Marchetti and Tocci 2011, 4). However, in increasingly interconnected political spaces, it is sometimes difficult to draw clear-cut distinctions between what is a purely local grassroots organization, a more structured NGO, or an international NGO (INGO). For instance, the organizations we have explored in this book are actually hybrids of more than one organizational form, developed on the basis of a partnership or partnerships created between local civil society groups and international donors, or with a network of other international civil society organizations. Among our three case NGOs, Partners In Health,

Haiti grew out of a local grassroots organization into an INGO with headquarters in Boston and branches in several countries. Women in Black–Serbia (WIB) and the Community Foundation for Northern Ireland (CFNI) are managed in their home nations, but exercise advocacy by participating in broader civil society networks and by appealing to a variety of donors, locally and internationally, for funding.

Defining the Need for Contextual Analyses of NGO Roles in Post-Conflict Societies

The reframing of international security as human security has resulted in an expansion of interventions into matters previously considered internal state concerns. The increasing interest of international organizations in directly intervening to protect populations from an array of dangers—from poverty to gross violations of human rights—has opened new spaces for NGO action, funding, and engagement. The United Nations (UN) Department of Peacekeeping Operations' 2008 *Manual for Integrated Peacekeeping Missions* recognized this changed reality by emphasizing the importance of coordinating with "the range of humanitarian and development actors involved in international crisis management . . . where the United Nations peacekeeping operations are deployed" (United Nations Department of Peacekeeping Operations 2008, 10). This reconceptualization of security reflects an emerging consensus among states, NGOs, and international organizations around what Oliver Richmond has called the "liberal peace": "a concurrent agreement between state and non-state actors on universal human needs, the provision of which brings a form of peace associated with world society" (Richmond 2005, 98). As the twenty-first century dawned, the UN conception of collective security had been reimagined and now includes cooperation with an increasing number of partners, including for-profit institutions and a variety of civil society organizations, including NGOs.

The ongoing redefinition of international security, the blurring of boundaries among participants in governance that it entails, the changing character of its actors and referents as well as the increasing role of NGOs in national and international governance it advocates are neither unproblematic nor uncontroversial (United Nations Department of Peacekeeping Operations 2008). Some analysts have praised this phenomenon as a signal of bottom-up democratization of the international system (Thomas 2001; Kaldor 2003; Lipschutz and Rowe 2005); others see the engagement of civil society entities in international politics as containing the seeds of a revolutionary possibility that will organize the "multitude" to bring down the capitalist system (Hardt and Negri 2000). Liberal and constructivist analyses of the work of NGOs and of community-based organizations of varying sorts have focused on their roles in mediating conflict; promoting social learning (Brown and Timmer 2006); and developing, linking, and bridging social capital (Edwards and Foley 2001).

Scholars inspired by Foucault, meanwhile, have argued that the NGO movement has been captured and now represents a liberal form of empire, aimed at containing migration and fostering rich nations' population security (Duffield 2007). Critics of interventionism to secure human security, whether through international government organizations (IGOs) or NGOs, contend it leads to the erosion of traditional state-based forms of democratic representation (Bickerton, Cunliffe, and Gourevitch 2007; Chandler 2009) that eventually, by externalizing political claims, delegitimize governments and thereby encourage international disorder (Badie 2000). Viewed through this lens, NGOs do not necessarily open alternative and more democratic ways of organizing politics, but instead represent another instance of security strategies aimed at containing the movement of people from poor to rich countries. However, beyond general calls for "solidarity," these critiques of NGOs have offered little analysis of the actual possibilities and outcomes of political action and change in the context of the prevailing neoliberal consensus (Duffield 2007; Richmond 2009).

In addition, with only a few exceptions, "in the literature, civil society has been normally discussed and analyzed in Western, peaceful, democratic and developed contexts" (Marchetti and Tocci 2009, 201). Because these circumstances cannot be assumed in post-conflict societies, such situations constitute an important but underexplored field for analysis and assessment of NGO efforts. As Richmond has argued, proponents of variants of a liberal peace, whether supporters of international organizations or cosmopolitan theorists, consider "civil society actors and their transnational connections as if they are divorced from the power of the state and norms of the international system" (Richmond 2005, 98). Indeed, "Within such debates there is an implicit acceptance of the norms and regimes associated with pluralism and democracy, human rights and social welfare" (Richmond 2005, 100).

However, the relative accuracy of such normative assumptions, their utility in post-conflict situations, and their potential for unintended effects merit further exploration. As Jens Sörensen has argued,

> In post-conflict societies, divided along ethnic, religious, or clan-based communities, the support of "civil society" in the absence of a *cross-sectarian idea of the state* may exacerbate fragmentation, either by supporting platforms for self-organization among sectarian groups or by generating conflict with pre-existing structures of solidarity; the selection involves a biopolitical separation into cohorts of population worthy of support, and cohorts to be excluded. . . . In a homogenous society where there is an over-arching idea of the state as the arbiter and ultimate provider of security, this provides for pluralism and an open arena of engagement. However, if the idea of the state is lacking, or if the state receives no instruments to attract cross-sectarian loyalty, while the space for competition on the market is promoted, such self-organization of sectarian interests may instead be a recipe for fragmentation. (Sörensen 2010, 78)

Exploring Rationales for Intervention: Good Governance, Risk Management, and Human Security

The UN adopted protecting people as an organizing collective security concept as the new century began, and with that shift human security emerged as a key legitimizing principle for international intervention in otherwise "sovereign" states.[1] Widespread adoption of a neoliberal understanding of government's functions and size has accompanied this redefinition. David Harvey has defined *neoliberalism* as a "theory of political economic practices that proposes that human well-being can best be advanced by liberating individual entrepreneurial freedoms" (Harvey 2005, 2). In this view, the state should play a minimal role in society, consisting principally of providing security for private property and promoting the functioning of the market. In practice, neoliberal policies promote and facilitate deregulation of markets, privatization of public services, and the withdrawal of the state from social welfare service provision. Burchell and Rose have each argued that neoliberal-inspired governance strategies delegate governmental functions to civil society organizations. In this framework, government is not, as in the welfare state, concerned with directly intervening to address or steer social phenomena, but instead delegates those functions to third parties (read: NGOs and corporations) and sets benchmarks and monitors their performance through accountability processes of various sorts (Burchell 1996; Rose 1996).

The neoliberal philosophy concerning how liberal democracies should be governed has not been confined to prescribing processes within states. In the 1990s it converged with other international conceptualizations that embraced democratization and human security as the main sources of legitimacy for international intervention, whether for peacekeeping or development. In line with this prescription and beginning in that decade, the United Nations embraced "good governance" as the political rationale for its interventions, whether aimed at democratization or peacekeeping, even as it defined "good governance" as "minimal governance," in accord with neoliberal prescriptions. Democratization was thereafter conceived as an asset of processes whose effectiveness could be gauged by well-crafted input and output measures. Because the neoliberal view calls for outsourcing or privatizing many government functions, UN democratization and peacebuilding initiatives in the last two decades have specifically engaged other actors, particularly NGOs, to perform previously public functions, especially those associated with providing services to states' most vulnerable citizens.

"Good governance" doctrines originated within the Anglo-American neoliberal critique of the welfare state (Schmitter 1997). R. A.W. Rhodes, for example, has identified at least six uses of "governance." These are "the minimal state; corporate governance; the new public management; 'good governance'; socio-cybernetic systems; and self-organizing networks" (Rhodes 1996, 653). The World Bank (the Bank), in particular, played a central role in elaborating the notion of "good governance" as a key organizing rationale for international institutions in the 1990s. The Bank defined *governance* as "the manner in which power is exercised in the management of a country's economic and social resources for development" (World Bank 1992, 92). For the World Bank, good governance for a state refers to "efficiency in public service, rule of law, especially for contracts, an honest and effective judiciary, respect for human rights and a free press and pluralistic institutional structures" (World Bank 1992, 92). The Bank embraced marketization of public services, reducing public sector staffing, budgetary discipline, administrative decentralization, privatization via contracting with NGOs, and increased public participation in governance politics as primary means to achieve these goals (Rhodes 1996, 656).

The UN definition of *good governance* mirrored this World Bank definition. The 1997 United Nations Development Programme (UNDP)–led conference on Sustainable Growth and Equity summarized key tenets of that entity's governance framework. The UN institution's approach highlighted the central significance of the regulatory role of government and argued that well-functioning states should occupy key roles in development. The conference viewed ensuring good governance—understood as "rule of law, predictable administration, legitimate power and responsive regulation"—as vital (United Nations Development Programme 1997, 5). However, for the UNDP, a state's task was not to provide services directly, but to develop an "enabling framework" through which private investors and service providers, including NGOs, could do so. The UN development organization argued that downsizing the state and emphasizing its regulatory and supervisory roles would pave the way to development more effectively than had previous strategies.

This emphasis on the central role of the regulatory function of the state has been crucial in UN elaborations of the good-governance doctrine. It was reprised, for example, in the 1998 Secretary-General's report on the role of the United Nations in supporting new or restored democracies (United Nations General Assembly 1998). In underscoring the World Bank's contribution to strengthening democratic institutions in new and restored democracies through programs of public sector reform, the secretary-general observed that the role of states must change from that of service providers to regulators, whose main function must be to enable market and "civil society" organizations to thrive.[2] Thereafter, promoting "regulatory states" became a central thrust of internationally led democratization initiatives. Ironically, this political rationality of minimalist government has been coupled in UN intervention mandates with a focus on institution-building. The result has been a prevailing political rationale that has assigned and entrusted NGOs with an increasing array of responsibilities, from performing as watchdogs for respect for human rights and political freedoms, to providing emergency relief to populations in distress caused by war or natural disasters, to serving as recipients of international funds for providing services to populations when governments are believed to lack the necessary capacity to deliver needed services themselves.

International security organizations' goals of fostering democratization and good governance converged with a reconceptualization of their task as reducing populations' exposure to risk of various sorts in the early years of the century's first decade. This turn in thinking and perspective has had marked results. In particular, the UN adopted risk as a primary organizing concept for its role in international security. Today's international arena has been reimagined at the United Nations as a web of complex interactions among a host of actors, resulting in diffused vulnerabilities and accountabilities and an overall reduction in predictability (United Nations General Assembly 2004). In this view, in addition to preventing or ending wars and ensuring the stability of the international legal order, the United Nations should promote human security. That is, the world body should intervene to prevent the spread of epidemics and famine, and should set up early warning and rapid reaction systems to address natural disasters as well as the disruptive effects of organized crime and nuclear proliferation. A variety of issues, previously dealt with separately, converged to form a new political rationality reflected in the UN High-Level Panel on Threats, Challenges and Change vision of the role of the United Nations in the new millennium. The panel conceived of the international arena as a risk society, international threats as shared vulnerabilities, and international security as risk management (United Nations General Assembly 2004).

As Ulrich Beck has argued, risk is both a social construct and a condition that derives from the intensification of connections among peoples and nations encouraged by globalization (Beck 1992 [1986]; Dean 1999).[3] In risk society, causal relationships do not follow linear paths, and the past is not necessarily a valid basis for predicting future outcomes. Beck highlights the danger of catastrophic events arising from increasing connections among people and states. Risk, he contends, is always a potential situated in the future, and therefore its evaluation and management are knowledge-intensive and rely on gaining accurate information concerning possible combinations of a diverse array of sources of danger. Beck suggested that since causal relationships and the effects of the interactions of a large and increasing number of variables are difficult to predict, security is now often viewed by national and international leaders alike as efforts to identify and control or eliminate factors that could potentially combine to generate catastrophic events (Beck 2009, 9–11).

Similarly, in the view of the UN High-Level Panel on Threats, Challenges and Change, all nations and their populations are at risk, regardless of their perceived relative standing or capabilities. No one is secure alone, and the ways in which risks may emerge are complex and therefore difficult to interpret and predict. The fact that insecurity is seen as both omnipresent and constant prompts policymakers to deploy a range of knowledge-intensive prevention strategies. In the United States, for example, this situation spurred passage of the USA PATRIOT Act in 2001, which curtailed a number of liberties in the name of addressing the terrorist threat the nation confronted.

For its part, the High-Level Panel broadened and redefined the notion of international threat to include "any event or process that leads to large-scale death or lessening of life chances and undermines States as the basic units of the international system" (United Nations General Assembly 2004, 8). More specifically, for the panel, international threats, broadly echoing the six components of human security defined by the UN Development Programme, included the following:

- Economic and social threats (poverty, infectious disease, and environmental degradation)
- Interstate conflict
- Intrastate conflict, including civil war, genocide, and other large-scale atrocities
- Nuclear, radiological, chemical, and biological weapons
- Terrorism
- Transnational organized crime (United Nations Development Programme 1994; United Nations General Assembly 2004)

This perspective treats state security and the stability of the international legal system as only one factor among many menaces to international order with which the United Nations must now concern itself.

Viewing international politics through the lens of risk challenges "container" theories of society, which consider territoriality the basis for the organization of political life. This analytic perspective creates new (and alternative) communities of danger (Beck 2000). Former secretary-general Kofi Annan's 2005 proposals for UN reform in favor of adopting a guiding human security construct marked a clear shift in the global body's goals and sources of legitimacy as a collective organization from states to populations. For Annan, while the United Nations remained an organization of sovereign states, international security now meant populations' security. States would continue to play important roles in efforts to realize that goal, but those steps would increasingly be instrumental in character (United Nations General Assembly 2005). For the secretary-general, "larger freedom," the organizing concept for UN reform as he envisaged it, included freedom from want, freedom from fear, and freedom to live in dignity (United Nations General Assembly 2005). Those ends, in his view, would only be realized by means of a holistic project for bettering conditions for populations around the world. Annan reimagined collective security as a comprehensive set of risk management strategies that engage multiple actors.

Whatever one's political assessment of the effects of this new view of international security as human security, this doctrine has certainly legitimized nonstate organizations to deal with matters traditionally considered the province only of states, intensified international willingness to intervene in what previously were considered a nation's internal affairs, and multiplied the number of relevant actors and stakeholders involved in peacekeeping and peacebuilding processes. This perspective has opened new spaces for NGO action, funding, and engagement. As a result, civil society organizations are seen as partners (for both international organizations and for relevant governments) in development projects, in institution-building, and in counterinsurgency operations.

Exploring NGOs as
Peacebuilding Actors in Different Contexts

The chapters that follow explore how NGOs engaged in peacebuilding efforts in diverse ways have sought to achieve the goals they set for themselves. We deliberately chose organizations that operate with very different missions and in different post-conflict situations. Our sample cases included an advocacy organization (Women in Black–Serbia), a service organization (Partners In Health, Haiti), and a community-based philanthropy (Community Foundation for Northern Ireland). Our aim was to identify how these organizations' understandings of their diverse roles in the post-conflict situations they have addressed have influenced the outcomes they produced. We found that organizations that continuously and critically reflected on their programming strategies, maintained scope for independent action, and did not prescribe rigidly defined outcomes were better able to achieve their goals than those that adopted other strategies.

The NGOs examined here have reacted in very different ways, and with markedly different consequences, to the opportunities and constraints opened by a political space in which neoliberalism, human security, and international interventionism now prevail. All of our case organizations—Women in Black–Serbia; Partners In Health, Haiti; and the Community Foundation for Northern Ireland—operate in post-conflict situations with strong international presence and multi-stakeholder peacekeeping or peacebuilding processes. The conflict scenarios in which each has operated and the international conceptualization of possible solutions were (and are) defined by a consensus that sees peacemaking as resulting from improving "human security" as well as "bettering" local governments. Nonetheless, that dominant view also often asks NGOs to act as de facto substitutes for government when the latter is considered unable to perform its functions. This has certainly been the case for Partners In Health, which has often undertaken the task of providing services that might appropriately be expected of the Haitian government.

The NGOs examined here assumed very different responsibilities and understood their roles in peacebuilding in very different ways. Women in Black–Serbia (WIB–Serbia) is a feminist advocacy organization that adopted the role of watchdog of the human rights–related performance of the Serbian government and aligned itself with the broader consensus of international and supranational organizations involved in peacekeeping in the region. In accord with that consensus, WIB–Serbia views promoting peace as rooted mainly in memorializing the victims of the Serbs, and in revealing the "truth" about that government's acts of violence. However, the overwhelming focus on memorializing the victims of conflict along state lines, combined with the adoption of ethically understandable but politically controversial claims, has produced the unintended consequence of contributing to further polarization of political identities in the Serbian nation's ongoing political debate.

Partners In Health, Haiti (PIH), meanwhile, chose instead to operate as a partner of the Haitian government and to try to employ the international resources it could garner in ways that not only would ensure promised services, but also help to build Haitian public sector capacity. Unlike Women in Black–Serbia or the Community Foundation for Northern Ireland, the primary focus of PIH is the provision of health care and related services to address what its leaders perceive to be the root causes of conflict: poverty and destitution. In Haiti, the international strategy of privatization of government functions by funding NGOs to provide basic services to populations has by and large produced a hodgepodge of assistance that has eroded such minimal capacity as that nation's government still possessed. PIH's experience suggests that it is possible for NGOs to achieve important results in rebuilding post-conflict societies. PIH has done so by designing its operations and services based on the needs of its clients, by engaging in continuous reflection on its program strategies, by protecting its operating latitude through diversification of its funding sources, and by choosing to operate in concert with local institutions—even when doing so increased service costs or required additional support to ensure its possibility.

The Community Foundation for Northern Ireland (CFNI) is a philanthropic organization that has operated within communities and neighborhoods in that nation with the aim of spurring dialogue among residents so as to catalyze the capacities of those with whom it works to create new ways of knowing and relating to one another that no longer involve persistent animus, mistrust, fear, or conflict. In Northern Ireland, despite international pressures to do so, the Community Foundation has not sought to demand adoption of a particular social vision by those groups and organizations for which it has provided support and with which it has worked. Its longtime director, who is also a scholar of Michel Foucault and therefore deeply aware of the "thickness" of narratives and contextual determination of meanings, has not taken for granted the apparent international consensus on grand rights discourses, but has worked instead to invite different groups and communities to voice their often divergent understandings of the outcomes they expect from the peace process. In this way, CFNI has worked not to create a "consensus" that obscures intercommunal differences, but a space where alternate interpretations of political outcomes may safely be voiced and contested and new meanings created. CFNI has secured its independence through funding diversification and has continuously engaged in critical reflection of its adopted strategies so as to learn from its missteps as well as successes.

A Brief Word on Methods

Our three analytic case studies rely on a combination of document analysis and semistructured individual interviews with our sample organizations' leaders and stakeholders. For each organization, we familiarized ourselves with its vision, mission, and programs as well as its approach to peacebuilding by examining its website, a wide range of documents and reports each has issued, and any other literature (academic or otherwise) we could find concerning its activities. We complemented this body of information with individual interviews, each averaging about 75 minutes, with a selection of leaders and stakeholders representing each NGO. These were selected first on the basis of their leadership roles, and thereafter by the time-honored practice of asking for referrals, or so-called "snowball sampling." We interviewed eight to 10 officials, whether NGO leaders, funders, or knowledgeable observers, for each organization we analyzed. We parsed our interviews for major themes and concerns, especially related to how each organization was seeking to position itself in its sociopolitical environment, its conception of peacebuilding, and its vision of the social change necessary to secure that aspiration and the appropriate processes by which it might be attained. We sought systematically to compare the strategies our organizations were pursuing against the contexts in which they were operating as well as against prevailing international claims concerning how they might proceed most effectively. We also sought to compare each NGO's efforts to those of the others we investigated. We believe this approach and combination of sources provides a rich contextual portrait of the intentions and motivations of each organization we studied and of the political, social, and economic contexts in which its peacebuilding efforts occurred.

Organization of the Book

This chapter has situated our aims and analysis broadly within relevant institutional trends and scholarship. Chapter 2 provides our analysis and findings concerning Partners In Health, Haiti. Chapter 3 contains our examination of Women in Black–Serbia's approach to peacebuilding in that post-conflict Balkan nation. Chapter 4 treats the Community Foundation for Northern Ireland's longtime peacebuilding programs and offers our assessment of that NGO's strategy. Finally, chapter 5 sketches our conclusions and shares what we have learned concerning NGO roles in peacebuilding, not only from investigating these three individual cases, but also from comparing and contrasting their experiences.

Irrespective of chapter, our analysis seeks to orient readers to the aims and historical background of each case organization we examine as well as how the NGO has conceptualized its role in post-conflict societies, how it interacts with funders and other relevant stakeholders, and what the perceived consequences of its adopted strategies have been for peace efforts in its political and social context. We seek, too, in each chapter to acquaint the reader with any broader implications of the case for theories of the roles of NGOs in international governance and peacebuilding, respectively.

Notes

1. This section draws on Zanotti 2010 (chaps. 3 and 4) and Zanotti 2005.

2. "The effort here is to help countries to redefine the role of the State, moving from a heavily interventionist paradigm to one in which the State's main function is to provide an enabling environment in which both the market economy and civil society can flourish. . . . The challenge is to reform the core systems of government, such as budgeting and financial management, the civil service, procurement, records management and cabinet processes. A special thrust has been decentralization, helping countries to define the functions best carried out by subordinate tiers of government, and to create a clear framework of fiscal responsibilities and limits" (United Nations General Assembly 1998, 3).

3. We accept Ulrich Beck's position that risk is both an emerging condition and a result of strategies adopted to manage insecurity.

2

Providing Services and Building the State Amid a Cacophony of International Aid: Partners In Health, Haiti

Health care does not exist in a separate universe from politics.
—Paul Farmer

The catastrophic January 2010 earthquake in Haiti not only caused 250,000 deaths and destroyed more than 80% of Port-au-Prince, the nation's capital city, but also delivered a serious blow to the thin layer of state administrative structures in place (International Crisis Group 2010). The crumbling of government buildings (all three branches of government and 15 of 17 ministries were destroyed) obliterated lives, historical memory, and part of the state archives, thus making management of both short-term relief efforts and the long-term recovery of the country even more difficult than it otherwise might have been.

Nevertheless, the earthquake did not create Haiti's weak state. That enduring concern had been addressed via international peacekeepers and aid for two decades. The object of these interventions has persistently been "state-building" and many analysts have blamed scarce state capacities on alleged deficiencies in the Haitian population or its government. Local factors, such as a lack of democratic culture, periodic political unrest, or some form of "savagery," have been identified as causes of the

A previous version of this chapter by Laura Zanotti was published as "Cacophonies of Aid, Failed State Building, and NGOs in Haiti: Setting the Stage for Disaster, Envisioning the Future," *Third World Quarterly* 31, no. 5 (2010): 755–71. Reprinted by permission of Taylor & Francis Ltd., (http://www.tandfonline.com) on behalf of *Third World Quarterly.*

fragility of Haitian institutions.[1] However, as one of the authors has argued elsewhere, after years of international peacekeeping and intense multilateral and bilateral aid as well as the continuing and intensive presence of NGOs in the country, attributions of causality that blame all that has gone wrong on the Haitians merit scrutiny (Zanotti 2008).

One notable factor that has seldom appeared in the literature as a serious challenge for institution-building is the long-term scarcity of economic resources available to the Haitian state. Instead, state-building has by and large been understood as an issue of the following:

- "Fighting corruption," which ultimately blames locals for their own challenges
- "Effectiveness" of international organizations, which frames the problem as well as its solution in technical terms
- "Training" of state administrators, which identifies "knowledge" as the main obstacle to be addressed
- "Institutional design" or "good governance," which ultimately disconnects the challenge of institution-building from its socioeconomic context[2]

As we noted in chapter 1, while the debates concerning NGO legitimacy and appropriate roles have been intense, the consequences (intended and unintended) of favoring nongovernmental organizations as service providers in the context of post-conflict state-building have received little scholarly consideration. The existing academic literature has focused mainly on assessing "effectiveness," or on exploring how to secure a measure of state oversight of NGOs without harming the latter (Richard and Mcloughin 2010; OECD 2008; Rose 2007, 2009; Sansom 2006; Van Slyke 2007; Vaux and Wisman 2005). The effects of delivering services through NGOs for building sustainable institutions in post-conflict or extremely poor societies have been little discussed.

This chapter argues that supporting NGOs instead of the Haitian state generally eroded, rather than reinforced, that state's capacity to act as a credible provider of resources to its citizens. In a situation like Haiti's, where the state can rely on very few sources of internal revenue, international support for NGOs in lieu of the nation de facto made institution-building unsustainable and compounded problems of governmental accountability to the electorate. However, we are also skeptical of overarching condemnations of NGOs as imperial "assemblages of occupation" and unsatisfied with generic calls for "solidarity" (Duffield 2007; Richmond 2009) as an effective guideline for policy in post-conflict societies.[3] Instead, we explore here how, practically, in the context of the neoliberal international consensus, extreme poverty, and a continuing lack of resources for state institutions to function effectively, NGOs may nonetheless be able to improve the lives of service recipients, while at the same time building the capacities of the Haitian state. Partners In Health, a locally accountable, internationally connected, and financially independent NGO, has demonstrated some success in securing just such effects.

Building Statehood Through NGOs: The Cacophony of International Aid and Intervention

As we previously observed, international organizations have since the 1990s conceived of efforts to build peace as strictly linked with developing state institutions and reengineering societies (Richmond 2005). However, at the same time, Anglo-Saxon social science has dramatically deemphasized the role of the state as an agent in development (Sörensen 2010). International institution peacebuilding strategies have converged with good-governance doctrines into a neoliberal philosophy that assistance should focus on the "democratic" form and "cost effectiveness" of institutional arrangements rather than on fostering state capacity to provide services to populations (Zanotti 2005).

Accordingly, NGOs have increasingly been considered relevant stakeholders in peacebuilding, both as alternative recipients of international funds (as opposed to governments as recipients) and as providers of emergency relief and long-term services to populations (United Nations Department of Peacekeeping Operations 2008). Before we examine Partners In Health and its specific efforts, we explore the international strategy of supporting NGOs to deliver services in lieu of governments and argue that such policies exacerbated the Haitian state's inability to perform its functions effectively.

Prior to the 2010 earthquake, there were between 8,000 and 9,000 NGOs active in Haiti with very different agendas, budget sizes, and sponsorship (Hallward 2007). These organizations operated in the context of a heavy presence of international multilateral and bilateral programs (through which they are often sponsored), a UN peacekeeping operation in charge of maintaining security and coordinating aid actors on the ground (the UN Stabilization Mission in Haiti, MINUSTAH), and a government with very weak administrative capacity. The work of NGOs in Haiti cannot be assessed apart from this context.

Paul Farmer, the founder of Partners In Health and now deputy to the UN special envoy for Haiti (former US president Bill Clinton), has argued that international assistance provided directly to the Haitian national government has always been limited:

> The aid coming through official channels was never very substantial: the US gave Haiti, per capita, one tenth of what it distributed in Kosovo. It is true that, as former US ambassadors and the Bush administration have recently claimed, hundreds of millions of dollars flowed into Haiti—but not to the elected government. A great deal of it went to the anti-Aristide opposition. (Farmer 2001)

This trend has continued after the catastrophic earthquake, as 98% of international aid provided since that event has circumvented the nation's government.

For its part, the Haitian state relies heavily on the foreign support it does receive for maintaining its operations. The national government obtains 70% of its revenue from external funders, and its independent capacity to generate income through taxation otherwise is minimal (International Crisis Group 2010). Thirty percent of the current state budget derives from customs revenues. However, the nation's main port at Port-au-Prince was seriously damaged by the quake, and in any case, Haiti's customhouses are controlled by special-interest groups (International Crisis Group 2010).

The nation's economic distress and dearth of governmental capacity is not new. Prior to the crisis triggered by the hurricanes of 2008, 76% of the Haitian population lived on less than two dollars a day, and 56% survived on incomes of less than one dollar per day. These figures had not improved by 2010. In 2006 fully 30% of Haiti's gross domestic product and the livelihood of about 1.1 million people depended on remittances from the nation's diaspora (International Crisis Group 2010). In the face of the increasing difficulty of making a living through agriculture (a process exacerbated by foreign food donations, as we argue), impoverished farmers have been flocking to the already overcrowded capital at the rate of 75,000 people per year. Prior to the earthquake, Port-au-Prince hosted 25% of Haiti's population, and 65% of those were poor and living in the city's slums. Of that population in poverty, 52% living in the city's slums, such as Cité Soleil, lacked sanitary services (International Crisis Group 2009). According to the International Labour Organization

(ILO), at least 90,000 jobs and 100,000 home-based businesses were lost in the 2010 earthquake, leaving about 1 million people without a source of income. Even before the disaster, the Haitian state provided few basic services to its people. For example, more than 70% of available health care was provided by NGOs, while 72% of the population had no access to health care at all. Meanwhile, 85% of education was provided by private schools, run mostly by NGOs (International Crisis Group 2009). Largely unregulated, these schools exhibit uneven educational standards.

Notwithstanding 15 years of international efforts to build the Haitian National Police (HNP), the United Nations continued to provide the major share of security in the country prior to the earthquake.[4] As of November 30, 2009, MINUSTAH included 9,065 total uniformed personnel, of whom 7,031 were troops and 2,034 were police.[5] November 2009 interviews with MINUSTAH personnel indicated the Haitian police remained heavily dependent on international resources for their recruiting, training, and operations budget. Training of new recruits at the Canadian-run police school was suspended in 2009 due to the state's inability to pay the salaries of additional officers. The HNP often lacks basic resources to conduct its daily operations, such as bullets for its members' guns or fuel for its (few) vehicles, due to external donor reluctance to support the agency's operating budget.[6] One result of this reality was the fact the force was largely absent from the streets of Port-au-Prince following the quake, suggesting clearly its institutional fragility.

International donors have for three decades considered channeling money through NGOs as a key tool of institution-building as well as a way of fighting corruption and fostering accountability. For example, in 1999, as a result of international discontent concerning a dispute over requirements concerning relative or absolute majority in that year's parliamentary elections, international donors withdrew all funds from the Haitian state as well as from the UN mission in place at the time (the Civilian Support Mission in Haiti, MICAH), and channeled assistance through NGOs instead. This strategy, however, has thus far not resulted in much stronger state institutions. Nonetheless, it seems clear that in the context of Haiti's extreme poverty and the state's continued lack of resources, this strategy de facto cut the lifeline to the process of institution-building that, ironically, served as the primary rationale for the international (UN) intervention in Haiti in the 1990s (Zanotti 2008). The disproportionate economic resources available to international organizations and NGOs as compared to the government, and the dependence of the latter on external funding to provide basic services, exacerbates accountability issues. The ability to secure support and funding through foreign NGOs has become a very important way for local political entrepreneurs to secure success. Since NGOs are basically accountable to the constituencies that sponsor them and Haitian government officials and politicians heavily rely on them to access the resources, financial or otherwise, necessary to provide assistance and services and to gain a measure of internal political consensus, the power of NGOs to steer and influence local politics is often stronger than that of relevant electorates.

Foreign states and political groups have also used NGOs to press their favored agendas in Haiti. In 2007, for example, about 70% of the funding available to Haitian NGOs was distributed by the US Agency for International Development (USAID) and the Canadian International Development Agency (CIDA). Furthermore, between 1994 and 2002 USAID, the International Foundation for Electoral Systems (IFES), and the International Republican Institute (IRI) reportedly contributed some $70 million to organize opposition to Aristide (Hallward 2007). Regardless of one's assessment of Aristide's performance as a statesman, these NGO-channeled interventions weakened the elected government, triggered instability and violent outbursts, and eventually fostered a coup d'état that ultimately prompted the (re)deployment of UN peacekeepers (MINUSTAH) to the country. In the context of the prevailing extreme poverty and weak state institutions, NGOs became "other governmental organizations," and their assigned roles, irrespective of any specific activities they may also have undertaken, contributed to eroding state officials' internal accountability and the possibility of building sound state institutions (Hallward 2007).

In interviews we conducted with them in late 2009, UN officials acknowledged that the massive withdrawal of funds from the government in favor of NGOs produced negative effects for institution-building. A number of UN representatives emphasized that the heavy reliance on NGOs had created a catch-22 situation. While these individuals conceded that given the government's continuing absence of administrative and economic resources, NGOs are essential to service provision, they nonetheless uniformly agreed that international support of NGOs instead of the government had created serious trade-offs with the necessity of building state capacity. For example, because local state salaries cannot compete with those offered by international NGOs, these organizations siphon skilled personnel from government posts. In this context, our interviewees suggested that UN or NGO personnel frequently carried out the administrative processes necessary for the government to function because the latter lacked staff to perform such tasks. The paucity of trained and professional administrative personnel available in the Haitian state has also made securing programmatic continuity during changes of government following elections very difficult.

The UN Economic and Social Council, realizing that international aid cannot be considered separately from institution-building, moved away in 2006 from the neoliberal consensus that has informed international political rationalities in the last two decades and prescribed that UN agencies work through NGOs to build government capacity (Economic and Social Council 2006). In line with this advice, the world body's agencies called for three-year strategic plans for their work with the Haitian government. However, several UN representatives underscored in interviews that these strategic plans had not meant much in practice. Regardless of what was established in the planning documents, in practice the government would follow the money and end up authorizing unplanned interventions if they came with funds. In short, in the 2000s, the Haitian national government began to suffer a fate often attributed to NGOs: it became donor driven. Moreover, even as UN agencies began to seek to reinforce locally elected government bodies by providing them direct aid, bilateral donors often sponsored NGO projects that created parallel structures, with resulting disruptive effects for constructing stable Haitian public institutions.

The presence of the United Nations has not materially reduced either the number of actors providing support, nor coordinated the ways and means by which they are doing so in Haiti. According to the *UN Integrated Peacekeeping Operations Manual,* UN peacekeeping missions should coordinate the work of all stakeholders in peacekeeping—that is, UN agencies and, indirectly, NGOs as well as the state and market institutions (United Nations Department of Peacekeeping Operations 2008). However, our interviews with MINUSTAH and UN agency representatives suggested that the task of coordinating and integrating diverse constituencies is far more difficult than appears in programmatic documents.

This is not necessarily due to a technical lack of coordinating mechanisms, but is instead typically the product of political differences in priorities and strategic choices. The UN country teams were relatively effective in coordinating the emergency relief interventions of NGOs and international governmental organizations (INGOs) following the 2008 hurricanes, but developing a long-term common strategy among agencies, peacekeepers, and the government to address Haiti's needs has proven to be a more difficult and elusive task. For example, while there is consensus among the various participating UN agencies in Haiti and MINUSTAH that it is necessary to go beyond provision of basic security and relief to promote peace and sustainable social and economic development, different agencies within the UN family have adopted dissimilar visions and strategies concerning how such goals might be attained. Some have supported the neoliberal program spelled out in Paul Collier's 2009 report to the UN secretary-general (Collier 2009), especially its export trade and goods focus, while others have favored agricultural development oriented to internal consumption and tourism promotion as a viable alternative to low-wage factory employment and export-oriented agriculture.

Internationally sponsored NGOs have been criticized not only for carrying out uncoordinated and particularistic political agendas, but also for being ineffective in actually delivering services and resources to Haitian citizens. For example, 84% of every USAID-provided dollar spent in Haiti—the lion's share of which is channeled through NGOs—returns to the United States in the guise of international experts' salaries, thereby contributing only marginal assistance to Haiti's population (Hallward 2007). In the worst-case scenario, INGO activities have purportedly actually damaged the local Haitian economy. In his study of CARE food deliveries in the fertile agricultural area of Jean Makout, for example, Timothy Schwartz concluded that food aid may have hampered local agricultural sustainability (Schwartz 2008).

Moreover, because a portion of CARE (and other NGO) budgets rely on the sale of donated food, selling such fare is essential for sustaining the budgets of the NGOs that distribute it. Since foodstuffs are donated to these organizations on the condition that they be offered for sale in local markets, civil society organizations distribute their donated crops and processed items in areas where there is infrastructure (capacity) to receive them, regardless of local production cycles or needs. In other words, food is delivered when and where it can most easily be exchanged for cash for the NGOs that provide it, not necessarily where it is most needed. Providing fertile areas with large quantities of internationally donated food during harvest season drives down the price of local crops and ultimately severely impairs the possibility for local growers to make a living from their harvests. Schwartz argues that despite the fact that local farmers requested assistance in acquiring refrigeration and storage technology so that their crops could be stored and thereby remain marketable longer, INGOs nonetheless continued delivering competing foods (Schwartz 2008). The massive increase in the flow of food aid after the quake strained the local economy, and in response, former president René Préval called for a halt to the practice and for redirecting assistance toward job creation instead (International Crisis Group 2010).

Emergency management efforts may also end up creating negative unintended consequences for local residents' capacity to provide durable services. While emergency relief INGOs are much needed for their ability to mobilize and provide support quickly when lives are at stake, their mandates are of limited duration and tied to crises. In consequence, these organizations may unintentionally create a void difficult to fill on their withdrawal. For example, in November 2009 Médecins Sans Frontières (MSF) announced its decision to withdraw from the trauma hospital in Port-au-Prince, on the argument that the emergency created by intense gang fighting in the slums was over and its services were therefore no longer required. Because the Haitian state did not have the resources to step in to provide services in MSF's stead, the question of whether and how assistance could be continued following that INGO's withdrawal quickly became significant.[7]

In addition, bureaucratic ownership and logistical issues may combine with mandate constraints and affect who delivers services and how to residents. For example, when MSF built a camp hospital in Gonaives following the 2008 hurricanes, the INGO demanded that its own personnel staff the facility. When the emergency ended and MSF withdrew, the problem of ensuring continuity of health services emerged as a critical one.[8]

In commenting in 2011 on post-earthquake relief efforts in Haiti, Farmer argued that moving from relief to recovery requires effective government oversight and coordination, which becomes very difficult if aid is provided principally by intermediary entities (Farmer 2011). Haiti's public institutions and international donors alike face what Farmer has labeled a tension between praxis and policy—that is, between providing immediate relief and basic services to extremely poor or displaced populations and implementing sound strategies for long-term economic growth and state-building. Farmer has asked, "Might responding to the acute needs of people displaced and injured by the earthquake afford us a chance to address the underlying chronic conditions that had rendered them so vulnerable in the first place?" (Farmer 2011, 22).

This discussion has highlighted the fact that international state-building strategies that privileged NGOs in lieu of the Haitian state as recipients of funds ultimately eroded the national government's already limited administrative capacity. That outcome has weakened efforts to nurture institutional capacity, stability, security, economic development, and the availability of basic services to the Haitian population. The catastrophic effects of the 2010 earthquake have only exacerbated this situation. It is therefore critical for reconstruction that international resources be directed to NGOs that not only are able to provide relief services, but also that have committed both to a long-term presence in the nation and to work with the Haitian government to create infrastructure, economic opportunities, and services. The argument that follows explores how Partners In Health, Haiti (PIH) has worked as an NGO in just this spirit.[9]

Achieving Success Amid Enduring Challenges

Partners In Health (PIH)—in Creole, Zanmi Lasante—was founded in the 1980s by Father Fritz Lafontant, Ophelia Dahl, and Paul Farmer, a Harvard University–based medical doctor and anthropologist. Their shared goal was to provide free health care to the poor living in Haiti's Plateau Centrale. The group was supported by a South Carolina Episcopal church organization that had worked in Cange since the 1970s to provide health care and schooling to families displaced by a dam built on the Artibonite River in 1956 as part of an international development project. The following excerpt from the PIH website describes the progress achieved since:

> The small community clinic that first started treating patients in the village of Cange in 1985 has grown into the Zanmi Lasante (ZL) Sociomedical Complex, featuring a 104-bed, full-service hospital with two operating rooms, adult and pediatric inpatient wards, an infectious disease centre . . . an outpatient clinic, a women's health clinic . . . ophthalmology and general medicine clinics, a laboratory, a pharmaceutical warehouse, a Red Cross blood bank, radiographic services, and a dozen schools. ZL has also expanded its operations to eight other sites across Haiti's Central Plateau and beyond. Today, ZL ranks as one of the largest nongovernmental health care providers in Haiti—and the only provider of comprehensive primary care, regardless of ability to pay, for more than half a million impoverished people living in the mountainous Central Plateau. (Partners In Health 2010f)

Put differently, PIH now serves as the primary provider of health care to the poor in a region that extends from Haiti's coast to its border with the Dominican Republic, an area containing approximately 1.2 million people.

PIH seeks to link academic research with social activism as it designs and provides medical care and its associated delivery systems. In addition to offering health-related services, PIH activities include training local doctors and nurses, using medical and anthropological research for sharing the results of state-of-the-art medical care with those who normally would not have access to it, and engaging in advocacy on behalf of the needs of those it serves. PIH leaders view health care as a fundamental human right, not a privilege (Farmer 2001). The NGO defines its mission as providing health care, alleviating the "root causes of disease" in Haiti and sharing the lessons it has learned in so doing as broadly as possible:

> At its root, our mission is both medical and moral. It is based on solidarity, rather than charity alone. When a person in Peru, or Siberia, or rural Haiti falls ill, PIH uses all of the means at our disposal to make them well—from pressuring drug manufacturers, to lobbying policy makers, to providing medical care and social services. Whatever it takes. Just as we would do if a member of our own family—or we ourselves—were ill. (Partners In Health 2010e)

This approach translates into five main principles for action for the organization:

- Providing access to primary health care
- Providing free health care and education for the poor
- Relying on community partnerships to provide services
- Addressing basic social and economic needs
- Serving the poor through the public sector

PIH's orientation to the provision of basic health care is a very important element of its success and a direct outcome of its leaders' understanding of the causes and treatment of diseases. Indeed, two principles for action, "providing access to primary health care" and "addressing basic social and economic needs," are strictly linked for PIH. For Farmer and the organization he leads, disease must be understood in relation to the patient's socioeconomic position (Farmer 2001). Diagnosis and treatment strategies take into consideration how poverty exacerbates risk factors as well as the constraints and limitations it imposes on the options available to patients for addressing their health needs. As a result, PIH health services are driven by a holistic vision that is rooted in and addresses a patient's life condition. While donor-driven health-care NGOs have typically undertaken the diagnosis, prevention, and sometimes treatment of the particular diseases they were funded to address (such as HIV), the needs-driven PIH, in contrast, integrates infectious disease interventions into provision of a wide range of basic health and social services. This includes not only the delivery of state-of-the-art medicines, but also provision of food (malnutrition has been identified as an important factor in the spread of many diseases) and, in some cases, monetary allowances to help families with ill members (Farmer 2001).

In addition, because of the obvious connection of malnutrition and lack of access to clean water to many diseases (including diarrheal illnesses and, more recently, cholera), Partners In Health has worked with other organizations to develop additional sources of potable water and more sustainable agricultural programs. In 2002, for example, it created Partners In Agriculture (Zanmi Agrikol, ZA), and ZA began a program to address the issue of malnutrition in the Plateau Centrale. In 2008 ZA assisted more than 5,000 malnourished children.[10] This outcome resulted from an integrated and holistic approach that, in addition to providing emergency food as necessary, developed family-based production. ZA provides farmers with tools and seed to cultivate their land and also buys seeds back from them each harvest. Purchased seeds are saved and donated to other families for the following planting season, thereby expanding the number of citizens with access to locally produced crops. On a broader scale, ZA shelters poor farmers from the vagaries of the market economy and aims to make the region more food self-sufficient. In 2008 the food price rise that followed an international oil price increase and the four hurricanes that hit Haiti that year reduced many in the nation to starvation. Haiti imported 80% of its foodstuffs before the quake in 2010. After the earthquake, food prices in Haiti increased once again, and thousands moved to the countryside from the destroyed capital to try to make a basic living. This reverse urbanization created a crisis in the nation's rural areas. In response, ZA identified crops that could be brought to harvest in fewer than three months and planted these on its own 80-acre farm as an example for area residents. ZA also expanded its provision of agricultural assistance from 2,000 to 5,000 families in the quake's aftermath (Dugan 2010).

Unlike many NGOs, PIH does not charge for its services. The organization believes strongly that health and education constitute keystones of development and must be provided free (Farmer 2001). Indeed, in situations of extreme poverty, PIH contends this approach removes a very important obstacle to access to needed sustenance or services. In addition to provision of free services, the principle of community partnership guides PIH's programmatic choices and its provision of health-care services. Furthermore, for PIH, "Funding alone . . . won't be enough. For this massive investment to make a real impact on the twin epidemics of poverty and disease, a comprehensive and community-based approach is key" (Partners In Health 2010d). In other words, for PIH, care must be rooted in the specific understanding of the particularity of the places within which it is delivered and provided in a way that addresses the needs of the people it is meant to benefit rather than meeting the demands of INGOs or NGOs.

Moreover, PIH views continuity of health services as critical. The NGO seeks to respond to the needs of the poor and is committed to partnering with local institutions to build local capacity to ensure ongoing provision of services. To a question in 2010 concerning whether PIH has an exit strategy, Ophelia Dahl, PIH director, replied,

> We don't. But we do have a transition strategy. Our goal is not to see how quickly we can leave a community, but to rebuild public health systems and infrastructure, provide training and support for local medical staff, and employ community health workers as agents of change to break the vicious cycle of poverty and disease. Over time, our success in achieving these goals reduces our role in providing direct service, but not our commitment. (Partners In Health 2010a)

Community health workers are central to implementing PIH's comprehensive approach to provision of medical care. These individuals increase access to therapy for individuals unable to reach distant clinics, monitor patient compliance with treatments, and provide disease prevention information and services. PIH also believes that community workers must be paid, and not, as many NGOs have elected, given food in return for volunteering work. By paying its workers, PIH routinely contributes toward creating economic sustainability in the communities where it operates (Farmer 2001). Increased community sustainability raises the chances that a given population will not fall into violence.

Partners in Health's choice to seek to provide medical services when and where they are needed, instead of asking patients to travel to medical facilities, proved very effective in ensuring emergency care for substantial numbers of people following the earthquake. For example, PIH has operated mobile clinics in four settlements in and around Port-au-Prince since the quake. These clinics treated nearly 4,200 patients during their first week of operation and have assisted with more than 100,000 medical encounters since their creation (Partners In Health 2010b).

PIH is driven by locally identified needs and thus is accountable to specific populations, but the organization is also part of an international network that makes transferring knowledge and financial resources from rich to poor areas possible. As Dahl has observed, the PIH model is based on its capacity to create partnerships at various levels, which buffers the NGO from external agendas and yet allows it to mobilize a considerable flow of resources. Unlike many NGOs that have worked beyond and in spite of the Haitian government, PIH has sought to contribute to creating local capacity by working cooperatively with the nation's public sector. As Farmer recently emphasized in a report to the US Senate Foreign Relations Committee, in order to be equitable and stable, health-care provision cannot be left to NGOs alone, but must be offered in partnership with the public sector (Partners In Health 2010g).

In more than 20 years of work in the Plateau Centrale, PIH has provided free health services and sought to promote economic and community sustainability by paying its workers and working through ZA to encourage sustainable local food production. The NGO has also sought to encourage social capital creation by equipping local residents with relevant professional skills and infrastructure to provide a range of needed services. For example, PIH now sponsors students to attend medical school. The NGO is now also constructing a teaching hospital in Mirabelais in concert with Haiti's Ministry of Health. It has also sought to encourage basic literacy through a network of 12 schools with the equivalent of kindergarten through grade 12. As Dahl has noted,

> Many of these young people have embraced a spirit of solidarity and a commitment to health and social justice. At a moving ceremony this past August, hundreds of people packed the Bon Sauveur chapel in Cange to celebrate and give a rousing send-off for seven students who are going to medical school in the Dominican Republic and Cuba. All of the students have pledged to return to the Central Plateau to serve the destitute sick after they complete their training. (Partners In Health, 2010a)

Conclusion

This chapter has argued that policies that have privileged NGOs in Haiti as favored recipients of international support have contributed to fostering the cacophony of aid besetting that nation, diminished and obscured the accountability of elected politicians to their local constituencies, and by siphoning human and monetary resources from the state, de facto jeopardized the building of sustainable institutions. Notably, to the extent an increased measure of sustainability is not attained, Haiti risks falling back into the conflict that has too often marked its history. Furthermore, because of the rigidity of their mandates or administrative processes, some major international NGOs have produced negative impacts on the local economy and on the durable and consistent availability of services to the population. However, while international strategies of privileging NGOs as principal providers of services have often not augmented state capacity and have created unintended consequences, not all NGOs can be dismissed as agents of new forms of imperial politics, or as detrimental to institutional and social sustainability and populations' well-being.

PIH's local roots encourage local accountability, while its connection to international networks of financial and institutional support facilitates the transfer of economic resources and knowledge from richer to poorer areas. The organization's diversified donor and investor population insulate PIH from undue influence by any single source of funding, governmental or private. Finally, PIH contends that economic security, politics, and human rights cannot be treated separately. For Paul Farmer and the organization he leads, the challenge of disease mitigation and eradication must be analyzed as a biosocial rather than simply a biomedical problem and addressed in the context of ensuring broader population access to sustainable economic and environmental resources, including food, clean water, and decent shelter.

Viewed as a whole, the history of PIH in Haiti suggests that NGOs that are locally accountable, needs-driven, and connected to a diversified network of local and international funding sources can create social capital, sustainable sources of income, literacy, access to health and locally grown food, and durable positive effects in the lives of the populations they serve. These factors are conducive to a more sustainable society, diminished risks for conflict, and improved prospects for enduring peace.

Notes

1. For a dated but still interesting review of these attributions of causality, see Lawless 1992. For a position that also emphasizes local factors such as "political culture" as a reason for UN failure, see United Nations General Assembly 2000.

2. For a critique of neoliberal conceptions that separated the institutional from the economic sphere in Haiti, see Cockaine 2009.

3. Duffield (2007) has argued that NGOs are part of broader assemblages of occupation. Both Duffield and Richmond (2009) have advocated solidarity as an alternative to international intervention and support.

4. The first UN Peacekeeping Operation with a mandate to reform the police (the UN Mission in Haiti, UNMIH) was deployed in 1995, after the elected president Jean Bertrand Aristide, who had been ousted by a coup d'état, was brought back to office by the United Nations. UN peacekeepers withdrew from Haiti in 2000, but redeployed there in 2004, after Aristide was ousted a second time.

5. At the same date MINUSTAH also included international civilian personnel, 1,212 local civilian staff, and 214 UN volunteers. After the quake, by its resolution no. 1908, January 19, 2010, the UN Security Council authorized an increase in the mission's strength to 8,940 military personnel and 3,711 police (www.un.org/en/peacekeeping/missions/minustah/facts.shtml).

6. Heidi Annabi, personal interview with authors, November 9, 2009.

7. We have not been able to determine what happened to this hospital in the 2010 earthquake.

8. Interview with a World Health Organization representative, Port-au-Prince, November 9, 2009.

9. However, the success story sketched in this chapter is not meant to suggest that PIH's activities alone have corrected the dynamics of the cacophony of aid at work in Haiti.

10. Interview with Gillaine Warne, ZA Cange, November 10, 2009.

3

Implementing the Liberal Peace, Hardening Conflict Identities: Women in Black–Serbia

> Belgrade, wake up! Belgrade, be ashamed!
> —Stasa Zajovic

This chapter explores the complex and often unintended consequences of NGO struggles to implement the normative claims embedded in discourses of liberal peace in post-conflict situations.[1] We examine Women in Black–Serbia (WIB) to investigate the tensions between WIB's adoption of a liberal, radically feminist, deterritorialized, and individualistic conceptualization of peace; its development of politics and political strategies in accord with the nationalistic identities it has purported to reject; and the organization of its advocacy for peace around memorializing war victims.

Richmond has argued that the liberal peace comprises a loose set of ideas and concepts, implemented through a web of actors in agreement on broad notions of democracy, the need for a market economy, and individual rights (Richmond 2005). NGOs help to establish the character of the liberal peace by the roles they play in negotiating with its various proponents and beneficiaries. Women in Black–Serbia operates in the aftermath of an ethnic war that divided what was once a multiethnic state, Yugoslavia, into six different nations. Some of those newfound states—Serbia, Macedonia, Bosnia-Herzegovina, Montenegro, Croatia, and Slovenia—contain areas ethnically cleansed during the conflict. International organizations (the United Nations, the Organization for Security and Co-operation in Europe), military alliances (the North Atlantic

Treaty Organization), and the European Union have played various roles in the war, in peacekeeping, and in the process of post-conflict reconstruction and peacebuilding in the newly formed countries.

For its part, the European Union has established specific admission criteria for these new nations and created the Stabilisation and Association Process to guide the transformation of their local politics as they move toward entry. As these efforts proceed, WIB–Serbia pursues its activities in a tense and ethnically divided context—heavily scrutinized and steered by international actors. The group has actively incorporated in its discourses and practices the central tenets of the liberal peace as the United Nations and the European Union particularly have developed that perspective. Women in Black–Serbia advocacy efforts also evidence some of the tensions inherent in the liberal peace between a state-based organization of politics and a universalist and individual-centered understanding of rights and identities.

Women in Black–Belgrade[2] was born of a transnational social movement. It seeks the remediation of specific justice claims arising from the war in Yugoslavia and envisages the development of a new society as the basis of their resolution. This chapter outlines how this radical feminist NGO organizes its political discourse, what instruments it employs to carry out its advocacy and political claims, and how its leaders relate to other civil society organizations and donors, the Serbian state, and international governmental organizations. Our analysis also assesses how, in a social and political context characterized by the persistence of conflict-related identities, nationalistic discourses, and heavy international presence, WIB activism produces both intended and unintended consequences.

We contend that the Serbian peace organization has embraced a liberal-cosmopolitan conceptualization of peace that resonates with the security discourses that have emerged at the United Nations in recent years. WIB skillfully employs various forms of communication not only for advocacy, but also as instruments to encourage healing among the Yugoslav War's victims. It takes advantage of the opportunities made available by globalization by networking across state borders with donors and other NGOs. It promotes connections and exchange of ideas among civil society actors, and it employs and fosters a nonterritorialized conceptualization of politics and political communities.

However, because WIB is widely viewed as supported by foreigners and operates in a political context in which nationalistic claims are frequently mobilized to counter perceived international interference, its largely liberal understanding of politics and peace is seen by its opponents as unduly foreign-oriented, unwilling to recognize Serbian sufferings, and too often willing to demonize the Serb nation-state. In addition, and paradoxically, we contend that some WIB discourses and strategies remain rooted in the national and statist identity the NGO otherwise contends it wants to protest and dismantle, and that its focus on memorializing the deaths associated with the conflict, while morally understandable, works instead to solidify, extend, and exacerbate the political debate around war issues. As a result, notwithstanding the important support that WIB–Serbia continues to provide to individual victims of the war, its advocacy claims often unintentionally harden the political imaginary of the community into its wartime identities.

This chapter does not treat the validity of WIB normative claims taken in isolation. Instead, we are interested in analyzing the effects that its declarations have produced in the complex political space within which they have been deployed. Indeed, political claims do not occur in a vacuum, and the linkages between discourses and the context in which they are pressed constitute a key dimension for understanding NGOs as political actors. Put differently, we do not endorse portrayals of WIB or the Serbian political space as marked by specific characteristics such as "nationalism," or WIB as an unambiguous promoter of the liberal peace. Instead, we analyze how the NGO's organization of its advocacy claims along the liberal peace consensus—in conjunction with its framing of guilt along national lines, coupled with its insistence on the memorialization of war crimes—contributes to further political polarization as well as to a concretization of Serbia's political imaginary into war-based identities.[3] More broadly, this analysis illuminates the unexplored conundrums, complexities, and ambiguities associated with implementation of universal claims in a highly polarized political space, and in the context of multi-stakeholder peacebuilding processes.

WIB, the Liberal Peace, and Post-Conflict Scenarios

Serbian Women in Black leaders describe their organization as a global network of individuals actively working to promote peace and justice while opposing all forms of war and political violence. They view themselves and their NGO as global citizens resisting patriarchy, nationalism, militarism, and fundamentalism. By emphasizing the priority of people over the state and by strongly rejecting nationalism, which these leaders see as connected closely with patriarchy, WIB has defined politics in ways that share some of the primary elements of the human security and "responsibility to protect" discourses that have redefined the UN approach to security in the new millennium. While we could not find a straightforward definition of *patriarchy* on the WIB website or in its various publications, WIB generally uses the term in connection with militarism, nationalism, war, and violence against women as well as in conjunction with broader discussions of social and economic inequality.

The published findings of a September 2006 conference titled "Security in Europe for Whom? Which Europe Do We Want?" sponsored by WIB illustrated how the NGO conceives these connections:

> The conference . . . brought forward inequality between men and women as a major obstacle to development of societies. The discussions uncovered the connection between male violence against women, patriarchy and gender power structures that sustain and perpetuate gender power misbalance. They outlined links between structures of violence in war and in patriarchal societies in "peace" whose faces are precariousness, unemployment, economic insecurity, trafficking and prostitution. The conference also highlighted the links between the global militaristic system and the patriarchal oppression and called for articulating and affirming ethics of care and a feminist platform of security through responsibility. (Women in Black 2006)

The origins of WIB–Serbia highlight the transnational character of the organization. While the issues addressed by the Serbian organization are situation-specific, the WIB global network shares the tools it employs to make its claims and to pursue its main mission. Women in Black began informally as an international advocacy network of women pacifists in 1987 during the first Palestinian *intifada*. In that year a group of predominantly Jewish women protested the Israeli government's occupation of the Gaza Strip. The number of WIB participants grew markedly in its first year of activity, and the enlarged group held weekly vigils in Tel Aviv and Haifa in addition to Jerusalem. Since its origins, this initially loosely organized association of women activists has focused on policy advocacy and relied on peaceful public displays and performances as well as on garnering mass media attention to obtain public awareness and salience for its perspective and concerns.

On December 2, 1988, to commemorate the beginning of the intifada, the WIB–Jerusalem branch organized a mass vigil in which more than half a million women participated. Israeli television and press covered the event extensively, and the program marked the official establishment of Women in Black–Israel. The organization quickly garnered international visibility and support, and WIB groups formed in the United States, Canada, Australia, and many European countries. On the heels of this growth, the scope of Women in Black advocacy expanded beyond the Israeli-Palestinian struggle to other national and international conflicts. During the first Gulf War, for example, WIB groups in the United States and Europe protested the US-led bombardment of Iraq. In 2008 the six Israeli branches of the INGO joined nine other Israeli feminist groups to form the Coalition of Women for Peace.

For its part, Women in Black–Belgrade was created in 1991 in non-violent opposition to the politics of the Serbian regime and the Yugoslav War. It established itself as an "active forum for women's voices and actions enabling networking, organizing, and campaigning for non-violent activism using public education, performance, and legislative initiatives" (Women in Black 2010a). Its overarching goal was to promote peace by pressuring targeted groups self-consciously to consider and redefine their prevailing values. WIB's efforts addressed not only Serbian government officials but also citizens supporting their actions. The mission statement of WIB–Belgrade evidences its liberal roots:

> As a women's feminist, anti-military peace organization, Women in Black practically and fundamentally:
> *Reject* all military power.
> *Uphold* the view that human rights are the utmost priority and take precedence to territorial sovereignty and state authority.
> *Demand* the separation of church and state.
> *Declare* the right to self-determination of all individuals regardless of ethnicity, orientation, or religion.
> *Advocate* the right and obligation of all people/society to monitor and hold government and individuals accountable for their actions.
> *Declare* the right and obligation of all individuals to participate in the peace process, and *Press* that women *need* to participate in peace negotiations and the peace process.
> *Demand* that international organizations take an active role in the peace process and recognize and treat women's rights as a key issue. (Women in Black 2010a)

As this statement suggests, WIB–Serbia emphasizes the priority of individuals' rights and the duty of taking responsibility for political outcomes. The NGO's mission embraces a cosmopolitan understanding of the universality of rights, promotes a vision of security that privileges people over states, and views civil society as the ultimate arbiter of policy legitimacy. Its discourse echoes the United Nations' conceptualization of security as human security, with its identification of the main source of legitimacy and referent for the organization's security goals as "the people." For WIB, "Security is the legitimate demand of each individual for the absence of violence, threats and fear and the protection of every human right. . . . Security is not about borders; it cannot be achieved with weapons. Just and lasting peace is the basis of security and it can only be achieved through creating a society in which all causes of war—including nationalism, patriarchy and exploitive economic systems—are eliminated" (Vuskovic and Trifunovic 2008, 182–83).

Similar to the Women in Black stance, and echoing the same liberal peace consensus, the 2004 Report of the UN High-Level Panel on Threats, Challenges and Change redefined security as human security and accorded sovereignty based on state performance. The panel argued that the right to exercise sovereignty fully should be conditional on a state's willingness and capacity to protect its people, thus legitimizing various degrees of international intervention when this condition is not fulfilled. In 2005, harking back to the preamble of the UN Charter, the UN secretary-general had also argued the source of legitimacy and the first referent of the United Nations as a security organization is "the people." Both of these arguments suggest that states are not automatically entitled to protection. Rather, such status must be earned. This focus on protecting populations in lieu of states, which have traditionally constituted the basic building block of the international legal order, blurs the question of who possesses sovereignty when and why, promotes multilayered governance forms and strategies, and ultimately legitimizes the United Nations to address populations directly (rather than states) through various instruments for monitoring and improving their lives.

With the advent of the twenty-first century, international security focused more and more on the optimization of processes of living together by developing more effective instruments for overseeing and controlling populaces. The United Nations and other agencies of international governance, such as the European Union, increasingly encouraged the collection of disaggregated data on populations, especially with regard to "vulnerable" groups. Thus, Resolution 1325 of the UN Security Council in 2000 recognized women as a special category of war victims, designated them as recipients of special forms of support, and argued that they were critical to the success of any peace process. WIB's focus on women as important actors in the peace process as well as special targets for humanitarian assistance suggests an embrace of the United Nations' growing attention to gender as a special analytical and operational dimension in conflict and post-conflict situations.

WIB–Belgrade officially views women not merely as key actors in post-conflict situations or humanitarian crises but as intrinsically better suited than men to foster and maintain peace:

> Women have always defended their homelands by their work—the raising of children, giving emotional and material support to the elderly and powerless, all through their invisible and unpaid work in the home. Therefore, we think that our attachment to and love for our countries (homelands) in general does not require that we espouse whatever view held by the army. We do not want to attain equality with men in that way. On the contrary, men must achieve equality with women by not exerting violence over women and not making use of the army, but rather through participating in the bringing up of children, in housework, to care for the elderly and powerless. (Women in Black 2010b)

For WIB–Serbia, feminism is a key tool for conceptualizing violence and for overcoming and breaking down the "patriarchal triad: sexism, nationalism, and militarism" (Zajovic, Perkovic, and Urosevic 2007, 71). Thus, "as feminists, we have the obligation to violate the imposed national consensus, because this is the only way we can work for peace" (Zajovic, Perkovic, and Urosevic 2007, 72). However, while feminist scholars' arguments concerning "maternal images" celebrating women as "nurturers and caregivers" have been successful in mobilizing women in peace movements, many of those same analysts have also pointed out that the assumption of the "inherent pacifism of women" reduces analyses of militarism to individual psychology (Tickner 2001, 59). Furthermore, an "ideology of women's essential difference" promotes a "biological reductionism that does not allow for change" (Tickner 2001, 59). As Tickner has observed, "In a context of male-dominated society, the association of men with war and women with peace also reinforces gender hierarchies and false dichotomies that contribute to the devaluation of both women and peace" (Tickner 2001, 59).

WIB defines politics in a nonstatist manner and self-consciously exploits the political opportunities created by the discourse of human security and increasingly interventionist international practice in support of the liberal peace. For instance, Women in Black–Belgrade, as previously noted, has creatively used the political opportunities provided by UN Security Council Resolution 1325 on women, peace, and security. While some members of the group have expressed skepticism of the declaration on the argument that peace cannot be achieved through military means, the NGO nonetheless has formally praised Resolution 1325 because it has "encouraged women to engage in new activities to deal with the problem of security" (Zajovic, Perkovic, and Urosevic 2007, 185).

WIB marked the fifth anniversary of Resolution 1325 by delivering a motion supporting it to the National Assembly of the Republic of Serbia. This move not only conveyed Resolution 1325 claims to the Serbian parliament; it also "localized" the resolution by applying its demands directly to Serbia, including its requests for full secularization of the state and application of family law, including condemnation of violence against women, revocation of the Law on Assistance to the Hague Indictees and Their Families, and criminalization of the denial of war crimes (Zajovic, Perkovic, and Urosevic 2007, 188–89).

In addition to pressing its national government for change, WIB–Belgrade also actively lobbies local, regional, and international constituencies. A case in point is its efforts to include the status of women in the discussion of the future of Kosovo. Women in Black shared its views concerning this thorny issue with the UN Security Council, the UN secretary-general, the Serbian Negotiations Team, the Albanian Negotiations Team, the Organization for Security and Co-operation, the European Union, the Contact Group, and the European Commission. Not surprisingly, perhaps, the NGO explicitly tied many of these advocacy efforts to Resolution 1325 (United Nations Security Council 2000). Among its other provisions, the resolution highlighted the need to address the special burden that women and children bear in wartime as well as their too-frequent marginalization in political life. Pointing to these twin imperatives, WIB–Belgrade volunteered the assistance of a team of women's peace networks to assist in securing an explicit role for women in the talks concerning Kosovo. While relying on Resolution 1325 as a means to press its agenda, WIB has nonetheless also distanced itself from some key UN strategies for making peace. In particular, Women in Black has consistently emphasized the need for ensuring the voice of actors besides governments in the Kosovo negotiations as a necessary step to confer legitimacy to the process.

Women in Black–Belgrade has employed public performances, book publication, and the organization of street vigils as key instruments to press its advocacy claims throughout its nearly 20-year existence. Indeed, during its relatively brief history, WIB–Serbia has organized more than 1,000 performances, petitions, public forums, and vigils. After the Yugoslav War ended, these events focused heavily on highlighting the accountability of national governments and international organizations as well as civil society institutions for human rights violations and crimes that occurred during the conflict. WIB–Serbia has coordinated traveling Women's Workshops across the Balkans to encourage public discussion of the human rights violations perpetrated during the war and how those might be acknowledged and some measure of justice achieved for those aggrieved. Women in Black has also actively monitored and publicized war crimes trials as these have unfolded, especially at the International Criminal Tribunal for the former Yugoslavia. WIB members have visited political prisoners and offered material and emotional aid to war-linked refugees and displaced persons. For example, during our visit to Belgrade in July 2009, Women in Black visited a gypsy community to highlight its displacement by the Universiades Games. The wanderers were reportedly not offered alternative accommodation by the Serbian government, and their freedom of movement was limited at night. WIB not only sought to provide visibility to the plight of the group, but also to create connections between the community and institutional actors that could assist them.

Whatever its specific political or advocacy claims, the NGO has sought self-consciously to employ public displays and media to extend its reach beyond existing state borders and bring its claims to the attention of a broader international audience. WIB–Serbia has often pursued its advocacy agenda by cooperating with other activist groups, with which it has established issue-specific alliances. For example, the group has long cooperated with DAH (which means "breath" or "spirit" in Serbian) Theatre Research Centre, founded in 1991 by several women actors and directors out of a shared need to create something positive amid the ongoing destruction of the war. DAH's first performance in 1992, *This Babylonian Confusion,* drew on songs by Bertolt Brecht as a testimony "against war, nationalism and destruction" (DAH Theatre Research Centre 2010). DAH has also worked closely with WIB to stage powerful vignettes based on the advocacy group's oral histories of women's family losses during the conflict. The Serbian NGO also connects on specific issue areas with other groups with different modus operandi, such as the Humanitarian Law Center, which provides legal support for war crimes trials.

WIB relies on a variety of funders, mostly on a project basis, such as interested individuals, local civil society organizations, regional organizations, and international organizations, as well as states to support its efforts. Among its sponsors are the Swedish women's NGO Kvinna to Kvinna; the Heart and Hand Foundation, San Francisco; the Women's Reconstruction Fund; and the Quaker Peace and Social Witness group, London. Thus, WIB's funding base mirrors its international aspirations.

This variety of supporters also testifies to the transnational character of the politics in which Women in Black is enmeshed and to the opportunities that international actors may have to shape civil societies by influencing NGO agendas through financing strategies. This globalization of politics, as we see in the next section, has also elicited nationalist criticism. Conversely, this situation also suggests the political opportunities available to NGOs to press their political claims by developing artful fund-raising skills and networks aimed (at least in part) at buffering funder accountability claims. That is, since these organizations possess multiple funders that seek accountability only for their specific purposes, imaginative management may allow NGOs to create operating discretion.

In addition to its range of advocacy activities, and in line with its individual-centered view of politics, WIB has actively supported women coping with the trauma of the loss of family members in the Yugoslav conflict by sponsoring activities aimed at promoting self-esteem, by facilitating connections among those so affected, and by making possible public testimonies by survivors of the ethnic cleansing and genocide. During and after the war, WIB supported women living in various refugee camps by providing activities that gave them at least some income and sense of self-worth. For example, during the siege of Sarajevo, when refugees began arriving in Serbia, WIB set up a knitting program in which supporters from abroad provided wool and women refugees made socks and earned income from selling them. According to the leader of WIB–Serbia, Sasha Kovacevic, this initiative gave the displaced women a sense of dignity and empowerment as each was treated as an individual and not simply as a member of a faceless mass.[4]

WIB–Belgrade has also used oral history and "memory writing" as a technique for helping women cope with the emotional trauma imposed by the war. Further to this aim it has published a book of oral histories of women who experienced life in the camps, titled *I Will Always Remember You.* In addition, in 2008, Women in Black published an anthology of women's testimonies concerning the war. The book was the result of a cooperative effort among several human rights and women's groups, and it recounted their direct testimonies with the aim of ensuring that the perspectives of women affected by the conflict would become an integral part of its history. WIB leaders believed strongly that long-term peace would be served by a thorough accounting of women's experiences of the war. Notably, the book of testimonies was supported by organizations outside Serbia and translated into English, suggesting that the NGO sought self-consciously to target an international readership, evidence of the group's ongoing strategy of internationalization and deterritorialization of political claims and alliances.

WIB has been successful in sharing and disseminating knowledge by gathering together different civil society organizations in educational activities aimed at raising awareness of human rights issues and the legacy of war. One example occurred during our visit to Belgrade in July 2009, when we were invited to attend a conference on transitional justice. Participants presented a number of different approaches to the matter of justice for those who lost loved ones to genocide or atrocities during the conflict. Presenters included, among others, Corinna Kumar, founder of the World Courts of Women, and Natasa Kandic, the founder and executive director of the Humanitarian Law Center in Belgrade. Kumar's and Kandic's institutions take very different approaches to justice. While the World Courts of Women have no legal ties, are convened by a community's "wise women," and seek reparation and emotional healing, rather than retribution for crimes, the Humanitarian Law Center in Belgrade has actively collected evidence on war crimes in the former Yugoslavia and strongly advocated for legal investigations and prosecutions of war criminals. The contrast in strategies between these participating groups is arresting, but highlighting their otherwise seemingly disparate efforts was nevertheless surely consonant with WIB's overarching aim of securing increased salience for its targeted concerns in Serbian society and beyond.

In summary, WIB has actively used the discourse of the liberal peace as it has been formulated by international organizations as well as the political opportunities offered by the changing definition of international security after the beginning of the new millennium. To do so, WIB has fostered cross-border communication and support networks in its areas of interest, has emphasized a universalistic and individualistic conception of human rights, and has contributed to a redefinition of politics as nonterritorial. However, as the next section suggests, its advocacy strategies and rhetoric have been framed by the very statist discourse it has endeavored to reject, and have been deployed in a very polarized and internationalized political context—a concern to which we now turn.

Political Advocacy and Paradox Amid Polarization

While WIB has adopted a strong antistatist and antimilitarist position, it has nonetheless organized how it supports the victims of war crimes according to national identities. The Serbian NGO's representatives explained to us in interviews that, because they are from Serbia, they feel compelled to apologize for the crimes of their own government, to support the victims of those atrocities, and to make it known that the acts were not undertaken "in their name" (the phrase "not in my name" has been employed by many protesting advocacy NGOs to point out the Serbian government's original complicity in the Srebrenica massacre). As one group member has observed,

> Asking for forgiveness is part of a tradition that is deeply rooted in this area. Yes, it is patriarchal, but we are changing this aspect of the habit. There (in Srebrenica), I am perceived as a member of that nation (Serbia). They see me as part of a mess that is not individualized, so when I go there as part of that mess, the first thing I must ask for is forgiveness. This is the first contact I have with these women, so the first thing I must ask for is forgiveness. (Harati 2009)

While it is ethically understandable, WIB's choice to support mainly the victims of the Serbian state ends up reinforcing the formation of identities along ethnic lines, and ironically thereby perpetuates the conflict that it is purportedly attempting to mitigate. Our experience in Potocari, the site of the Srebrenica massacre, illustrates this point. It also helps to illuminate the context within which the NGO's actions are conducted and to point out the enduring legacy of the war for the configuration of political and geographic space and people's identities.

In July 2009 we traveled in a group organized by WIB from Belgrade to Potocari to participate in a ceremony remembering the systematic murder of more than 8,000 Muslim men, who were drawn by Radko Mladic's Serb paramilitary forces from the UN buildings where they had sought refuge.[5] WIB–Belgrade participants were joined by members of WIB–Italy and WIB–Spain, the staff of the Humanitarian Law Center, and representatives of the Swedish organization Kvinna to Kvinna, together with a handful of other activists. The road to Srebrenica is bordered by homes that evidence the shelling and gunfire that befell the area in the war, and by cemeteries, mostly Serb, marked by dark marble Orthodox crosses. These burial grounds vary in size, some amounting only to family plots, while others include hundreds of graves. International aid for reconstruction was also evident. More than 90% of the houses have evidently been recently refurbished or rebuilt.

The site of the commemoration is difficult to describe. The abandoned UN buildings, now used in part for a museum commemorating the victims, are located in an otherwise beautiful high-mountain valley along a narrow country road. The gravesites of the massacre's approximately 3,000 victims who have been identified to date are located across the road from the old UN compound. Identification of remains and burials continue 15 years after the killings. On July 11, 2009, for example, we witnessed the burial of 534 victims identified through ongoing internationally supported forensic investigations.

The cemetery occupies the entire side of a hill and is situated in a territory that historically had been occupied by a mix of Muslims, Jews, and Orthodox, but which was ethnically cleansed during the war and is now largely Serb and Serbian Orthodox. The wide expanse occupied by thousands of white columns that mark the graves of the murdered offers a moving visual reminder of the atrocities that took place nearby. Thousands of Muslims attended the ceremony. Security personnel heavily patrolled the several-kilometers-long lines of cars and buses on the way to the burial site. Officials from the European Union and the United States,[6] in addition to Islamic religious authorities and local political representatives, were also present. WIB constituted a very visible presence in support of the victims. Organization members, in line with its strategy of relying heavily on performance and symbolic communication to carry out its advocacy, comprised a first line close to the dais, with dozens of WIB representatives dressed in black, carrying flowers and signs expressing solidarity for the victims and demanding the Serb government institute a national day of remembrance of Srebrenica.

Following the ceremony and not long after our departure, our bus stopped at a restaurant along the road, located in the vicinity of a Serb cemetery. At that location our waiter, a Serb man in his 20s who treated all of us very courteously, asked a question that was in many ways revealing of the potentially problematic unintended consequences of the WIB advocacy strategy and of the internationally supported commemoration effort as a whole. "Why," he asked, "don't you come back tomorrow, when we will commemorate our dead?" One might dismiss this question as another example of Serb denial of the many atrocities committed during the war. However, while not condoning the stance of denial supported by radical groups in Serbia, we decided to take the waiter's question seriously and to explore the position and response of representatives of Women in Black to the young man's query. In fact, while the number and way the Muslims were killed by Mladic militias was disproportionately large and vicious, the war also saw a number of Serb victims of Muslim paramilitaries in the area.

Ironically, while rejecting the state as a valid criterion for defining its own identity ("not in my name") and by decrying its violent manifestations, WIB–Serbia nonetheless, by choosing to employ belonging to the Serb state as the measure for selecting which dead are to be supported and legitimized, is perpetuating and reinforcing the identities at play in the conflict. Perversely, perhaps, while the moral claim of securing remembrance and justice for these victims that guides the WIB is surely praiseworthy, the political consequences of such choices contradict the central goals of the organization. Because Women in Black seems to have accepted the structure of state power as a valid criterion for deciding between the victims to be supported and the ones to be forgotten, the NGO has involuntarily ended up reinforcing the oppositional identities it purports to loathe. Coupled with the large (yet unfortunately only post-facto) international support for the Muslim victims, WIB's choice provides Serb nationalistic groups (or constituencies) an opportunity to claim that their nation is the victim of an international conspiracy. The group's choice to be present for the Muslim (but not Serb) victims in Srebrenica, while justifiable given the enormity of the atrocity perpetrated by Mladic, nonetheless has served to reinforce Serb feelings of victimization by the local and international communities. The choice to apologize only to the victims of the Serbian state has created the unintended consequence of contributing to strengthening the polarized identities fueled by the Yugoslav conflict.

Several of the people we interviewed during our field visit to Serbia pointed to the difficulties implicit in conducting advocacy in a highly polarized situation. Some indicated that offering equal support to Serbian victims as well would expose WIB to the risk of being exploited by Serb nationalistic discourses.[7] A Women in Black intern also expressed this concern. As she has indicated in her blog, two representatives of WIB–Serbia attended the August 4, 2009, commemoration of the Serb victims of Operation Storm in 1995 in Croatia.[8] There, reportedly, the principal speaker used the opportunity to politicize the issue and link it to a call for Kosovo's independence.

WIB's choice to support the Serb victims of Croatian forces (while with a much smaller presence than at Srebrenica) as well as its support for the Regional Fact-finding Commission (RECOM) on the Victims of Wars in Former Yugoslavia—a civil society–based initiative aimed at establishing and maintaining records of all crimes committed during the war that resulted in the breakup of the former Yugoslavia—suggests that WIB is attempting to navigate ways of organizing its advocacy regarding the memorialization of war crimes between a focus on victims of the Serbian state and a more regionalized and individual-focused strategy of commemorating the war deaths.

The debate concerning RECOM's establishment and its potential effects on social reconciliation points out the complexities and dilemmas connected with victim advocacy and memorializing war crimes in highly polarized political contexts. The drive to create RECOM has been led by Humanitarian Law Center director Kandic, funded by the National Endowment for Democracy, and supported by the European Union and some 400 additional national and international NGOs. RECOM's proponents contend that individualizing the memory of crimes would offer a path to reconciliation, on the view that such a process would avoid casting blame on specific nationalities and that "telling the truth" would prevent similar horrors from happening again. Bogdan Ivanisevic, a consultant to the International Center for Transitional Justice, has neatly articulated this position: "As a government and multilateral body . . . [RECOM] could be effective. Governments themselves would run the commission and promote it through mutual agreements, thereby reducing the risk of it being demonized. No one could say it was 'anti-Serb,' 'anti-Albanian,' etc." (Ferrara 2010). RECOM opponents, meanwhile, maintain that by depoliticizing and relativizing the atrocities committed during the war, the commission would effectively support the politics of denial that some groups within Serbian society embrace. Thus, Sonja Biserko, president of the Helsinki Committee for Human Rights in Serbia, has criticized RECOM on the grounds that a regional approach to confronting the past built on individualizing crimes would obscure the fact the atrocities committed in Bosnia-Herzegovina "were not organized in the name of their individual characteristics, but in terms of an imagined Serb group identity" (Biserko and Becirevic, 2009). For Biserko, a RECOM regional approach would only strengthen the hand of those who deny Serbian responsibility for wartime massacres, and therefore would end up actually impeding genuine reconciliation. In addition, Kandic has noted that while promoting a regional approach to the issue of war crimes is aimed at taming nationalistic representations of the war, the Serbian government's promised cooperation with RECOM has been carefully parsed, selective in character, and organized along nationalistic lines—that is, supportive when the "indicted or suspects are non Serb" (B92 2010a).

While supporting the controversial RECOM initiative may indicate a conscious attempt by WIB to redefine its strategies away from nationalistic criteria for the documentation of war crimes, most of its activities have remained targeted to commemorating the victims of the Serbian state. In addition, the fierce debate about which victims should be included in the process of documentation signals that RECOM's focus on documenting war crimes victims has produced increased political polarization rather than reconciliation.

A similar trend is evident in the debate that surrounded the establishment of a Srebrenica commemoration day. WIB advocacy on behalf of establishing a memorial day to honor those massacred, coupled with international political pressure, successfully secured adoption in March 2010 of a resolution by the national Serb parliament condemning the murders at Srebrenica, apologizing to the families of the victims, and advocating cooperation with the International Criminal Tribunal for the former Yugoslavia. The Serb resolution also called for other governments in the region to follow suit by recognizing and apologizing for crimes against Serbs. The debate and public opinion polls concerning the resolution pointed up the divided political climate. The controversy also exposed the potentially very divisive effects of continuing to promote peacebuilding by focusing mainly on memorializing victims. Another example is seen in a 2010 poll conducted by the Organization for Security and Co-operation in Europe and the Belgrade Center for Human Rights, in which responses suggested that 65% of Serbs opposed arresting the commander of the forces responsible for the Srebrenica massacre, Ratko Mladic, and only 25% believed he should be taken to the Hague for trial (B92 2010b).[9]

The debate in the Serbian parliament and in the press concerning the Srebrenica resolution also revealed profound disagreement among NGOs, citizens, and parliamentarians regarding what is and is not conducive to reconciliation. Kandic, of the Humanitarian Law Center, and other activists—including members of the Mothers of Srebrenica, a group that WIB strongly supports—saw the omission of the word "genocide" from the resolution as an indicator of a lack of political will to respect the victims and therefore as an obstacle to reconciliation. But Serb Radical Party parliamentary group chief Dragan Todorovic viewed the Srebrenica resolution as yet another example of the demonization of Serbs. As he observed, "Primarily because of the crimes committed against Serbs, those who committed them make declarations, but how can we ask them to make statements about the crimes when, for example, Croatia celebrates operations Storms and Flash, where the biggest ethnic cleansing in Europe was committed after World War II?" (B92 2010c). In this perspective, the most significant obstacle to reconciliation is not insufficient condemnation of the Srebrenica Massacre, but a systematic lack of recognition for the suffering of the Serb people, as Liberal Democratic Party leader Cedomir Jovanovic emphasized during debate concerning the resolution (B92 2010c).

The divisive effect of some WIB–Serbia public advocacy was confirmed for us during our visit in 2009 in the context of a silent, peaceful performance we observed staged in Belgrade to demand the institutionalization of a Serbian day of remembrance for Srebrenica and to lay flowers in a public square near the state capital. Members of Obraz, an extremist group whose members displayed large pictures of Mladic and Karadzic, surrounded the vigil site and shouted insults and murder threats at the WIB representatives. Heavily armed Serbian police escorted the WIB group from the organization's offices to the vigil site and separated the protestors from Obraz members. Apart from the small crowd of angry extremists, passersby seemed to be largely indifferent to the event. Not many stopped to show support for either group. The upshot of the effort seemed to confirm WIB adherents in their aims while reinforcing Obraz members in their own.

Public comments on the actions of the NGOs supporting the Srebrenica resolution published on the B92 newspaper website also illustrate the debate's discordant political effects. A few examples suggest the character and depth of the divisions at play. One reader's comment, "It is these NGOs that are the voice of consciousness in Serbia and listening to them can only bring about improvements in the country," prompted the following response: "These NGOs are all lavishly financed by NATO-bloc countries and the only voice they speak with is that of their American Masters" (B92 2010d). Another reader who observed, "The Humanitarian Law Center, Women in Black, Helsinki Human Rights Committee in Serbia, the Center for Improving Legal Studies . . . these are among the brightest in Serbia, and I thank each and every one of you. . . . Someone has to stand in for Serbia's conscience," received this response: "NGOs are all US/EU sponsored organizations, or some would even call them havens for spies. Then little wonder they are calling for the so-called Srebrenica memorial day." In referring to Kandic, another commentator on the site noted, "The victims should receive justice, all victims. Her problem is that she is too obsessed with non-Serbian victims" (B92 2010c).

As these examples indicate, the Serbian debate on political responsibility for the war and its crimes is rendered more complex by the conditionality connected to the process of EU accession and by the strong role of the European Union, the United States, and other international actors in constructing the accepted narrative or imaginary of the war. The conditions imposed by the European Union on Serbia concerning cooperation with the International Criminal Tribunal for the former Yugoslavia and its own processes, the strong support of the National Endowment for Democracy for RECOM, and the activities of various activist NGOs do in some instances offer fertile soil for those who would interpret Serbia's recent history as a helpless victim of international pressure and demonization. A poll conducted by the Gallup Balkan Monitor in July 2010 indicated the percentage of people in Serbia who believed joining the European Union would be good for their country had dropped from 50% to 44%. In that same poll, only 13% of Serbs favored joining NATO, while 52% opposed doing so. In addition, while 64% of the poll's participants believed that relations with neighbors should be reinforced, 24% perceived there would be a new round of war. Residents of Croatia, Macedonia, and Albania have evidenced a similar decline in enthusiasm for joining the European Union in recent polling, while the trend of support for membership among residents of the West Balkan countries and Kosovo is positive (B92 2010b).

The language used by Serbian president Boris Tadic in expressing his support for the Srebrenica resolution, which targeted an international audience while maintaining awareness of local nationalistic sentiments, illustrated the complexity of the political terrain he sought to navigate. On the one hand, Tadic linked parliamentary passage of the resolution to the benefits awaiting the nation with EU access: "This resolution," Tadic declared, "speaks clearly on the political values of Serbia and how we see our region, our neighbors and our united European future" (B92 2010e). On the other hand, in an apparent bid to quell nationalistic ferment, Tadic added that adoption of the resolution was not the result of international pressure, but an independent choice that reflected Serbian values. Rasim Lalic, minister of labor and social policy, echoed Tadic's comments when he noted that Serbia adopted the Srebrenica resolution "because of its own interest, and by that the country claimed the right to the place it is entitled to as the leading regional country" (B92 2010e).

Conclusion

This chapter has explored the work of WIB–Serbia not only with respect to its normative claims, but also with regard to the political consequences that those advocacy demands have produced in the highly internationalized and polarized post-conflict political context in the Balkans. We have argued that the WIB advocacy posture and strategy highlight the increasing internationalization of politics and the connections between radical NGO discourses and what are considered "mainstream" conceptualizations of peace and security produced by international organizations such as the United Nations and the European Union. Women in Black–Serbia generally has been skillful in mobilizing sponsors and activating networks concerning issues it seeks to bring to public attention. WIB's concern to secure justice for those wronged by the atrocities of the war makes the organization a natural ally of the individualist claims that underpin calls for the liberal peace. We have suggested that, in the complex political context of a post-conflict society, this blending of the normative claims of the liberal peace and the internationalization of politics they promote, together with the organization of victim support along statist lines, have contributed to creating the ironic political effect of reinforcing conflict identities. These effects have been assessed against the complex political space of the Balkans and Serbia in particular.

The contested nature of how to create conditions for peace in a polarized postwar political environment is evident in the ambivalent and ambiguous interpretations of the RECOM process, for some a beacon of war because it relativizes crimes, while for others an instrument of peace because it is seen as making justice possible. This divergence is also evident in the competing interpretations of the institutionalization of a Srebrenica commemoration day. For some the establishment of such a memorial represented yet another instance of the international victimization of Serbs and the uneven recognition of crimes committed during the war; for others that remembrance did not go far enough, and the fact that the Srebrenica massacre was not called a genocide represented yet another example of a Serbian national denial of responsibility for the killings. Regardless of these different positions, the continuous focus on the horrors of the war, fostered by the internationally supported effort in which WIB takes active part with its own claims oscillating between the liberal peace and a nationalistic stance, may end up hardening identities along the lines of victims/perpetrators (regardless of who may claim either role), and offering room for exploitation of advocacy initiatives by radical warmongering groups.

In summary, in a heavily internationalized political space that includes multiple stakeholders (the United Nations, the European Union, NATO, and NGOs, as well as national politicians and populations), the effects of NGO-driven normative claims regarding guilt and justice need to be carefully assessed. This is true especially when the latter is framed along the lines of national identities, combined with the focus of advocacy for peace around the memorialization of war atrocities. In the absence of more comprehensive ways of encouraging alternative identities and political imaginaries, assuming that the recounting of suffering and the counting of the deaths will lead to a more peaceful society is just too simplistic. The expansion of what is considered the legitimate space for governance beyond state borders, the multiplication of stakeholders that claim legitimacy in political processes, and the hybridization of their identities between the local and transnational add elements of complexity to the assessment of the political effects of advocacy claims that, while resonating with the accepted consensus of the liberal peace, may result in unintended consequences when they claim for themselves universal validity in a polarized political space.

This chapter has explored these complexities, and sought to provide a more nuanced analysis of an exemplar NGO and thereby help to develop more effective international strategies for building peace that should consider the complex effects of the interactions between narrowly defined normative claims and local politics and dynamics. As David Kennedy has stated in his work on international humanitarianism,

> We have treated our norms as true rather than as reminders of what might be made true. We have substituted multilateral decisions for humanitarian decisions, and the work of the United Nations for humanitarian work. We have mistaken a pragmatic vocabulary of instrumental reason for responsibility. The idolatry of tools disguises itself as the wisdom of the long run. But let us assess those long-term promises with cold and disenchanted eyes. (Kennedy 2004, 20)

Universal human rights claims should be carefully evaluated in the political, economic, and social contexts in which they are advanced, as instruments that produce specific outcomes. Those effects determine trajectories for peace.

Notes

1. A previous version of this chapter was published as Max Stephenson Jr. and Laura Zanotti, "Implementing the Liberal Peace in Post-Conflict Scenarios: The Case of Women in Black–Serbia," *Global Policy* 3, no. 1 (February 2012): 46–57. Reprinted with permission.

2. Hereafter, following the group's own practice, we use "Women in Black," "WIB," or "Women in Black–Serbia" to refer to this civil society advocacy group.

3. A thorough discussion of identities formation in the Balkans is beyond the scope of this chapter. For a critical discussion of the Western representation of the Balkans as coded along nationalistic lines, and for a study of the competing ideologies that have contributed to form identities, see Hatzopoulos 2008. For a different analytical perspective on Serb identity and pan-Yugoslavism, see Bulatovic 2004. Here we embrace Hatzopoulos's invitation to look at the Balkans as a political space undergoing complex transformations. By analyzing the effects of political claims in context, we seek to avoid dichotomizing the identities in play.

4. Sasha Kovacevic, personal interview with authors, 2009.

5. See United Nations 1999. Chilling footage on the Srebrenica massacre, mostly recorded by Mladic paramilitary force members, is available on YouTube, as are several other short films detailing the tragic events. See www.youtube.com/watch?v=c95xiE-_o1Q&feature=related.

6. The US ambassador Charles English as well as US congressman Michael Turner, from Dayton, Ohio, and his wife participated in the commemoration.

7. Interview by authors with Anna Lidstrom, country coordinator for Serbia and Montenegro of Kvinna to Kvinna, Belgrade, July 2009.

8. In 1995 the Croatian government army recovered part of the territory lost to the Krajina Serbs who had previously declared independence from Croatia, through two military operations: "Flash," which regained western Slavonia in May, and "Storm," which regained the areas known as UN Sectors North and South in August. In the process, although exact figures are still disputed, best estimates suggest around 2,000 Serbs were killed, an estimated 1,200 of whom were civilians. Approximately 20,000 Serb-owned homes in Croatia were burned (as reported by Donna Harati, http://advocacynet.org/wordpress-mu/dharati/). August 4 is celebrated in Croatia as the Day of Gratitude to the Homeland Defenders.

9. Ratko Mladic was apprehended and arrested without incident on May 26, 2011, and later extradited from Serbia to the Hague to stand trial for war crimes. See BBC 2011 and Marlise Simon, *New York Times,* May 31, 2011.

4

Revealing Conflict Narratives in Pursuit of Peace: Exploring the Peacebuilding Efforts of the Community Foundation for Northern Ireland

It's not just about funding, it's about how big your imagination is.
—Avila Kilmurray

The Belfast, or Good Friday, Agreement of 1998 launched a new "post-Troubles" era in Northern Ireland that has witnessed a concerted series of efforts by the province's reconstituted government, by the government of the United Kingdom, by the European Union, and by a variety of civil society organizations to address the conditions that led to more than 30 years of protracted ethnic and sectarian violence and more than 3,500 deaths (Aiken 2010, 172). These entities have sought to develop mechanisms to address the complex array of social concerns, cultural characteristics, and political and economic conditions that had led to social violence for so long, so as to enable the region's nearly 2 million residents to move forward in peace. Even a partial listing of the array of concerns that have confronted and continue to challenge these would-be peacebuilders is daunting:

- Pockets of long-standing poverty in the province and in the cross-border region with the Republic of Ireland, and relative deprivation in many of Northern Ireland's communities and neighborhoods
- Persistent, although declining, social and income inequality between better-off Protestant versus Roman Catholic ethnic groups
- Profound and continuing residential segregation between the primary antagonistic groups

- Lingering distrust among members of ethnic groups in many communities, especially those in which many lives were lost in the period of violence
- Nearly uniform single-identity education—for example, Protestant and Catholic schools educating the children of adherents separately
- Little or no consensus on a shared narrative of the genesis and responsibility for the Troubles among various institutions and population groups in Northern Ireland[1]
- A continuing strong sense of victimhood among members of primary ethnic groups that extends only to their own members

Given these manifest complexities, we do not pretend here to enter into an exhaustive analysis of these dynamics, or even into a comprehensive examination of how the Community Foundation for Northern Ireland (CFNI) has engaged them over the ensuing period. Rather, we seek to delimit the peacebuilding roles that the foundation has undertaken as it has focused on the narratives at play in sustaining the conflict and in promoting reflection on their meaning and consequences for conflicting groups. We examine how CFNI efforts relate to the broader debate concerning the potential agency of NGOs in international politics as well as to a reconceptualization of peacebuilding as continuous engagement, rather than as an initiative with predefined outcomes.

We recognize that CFNI is one of several NGOs that have played long-term and vital roles in peacebuilding in Northern Ireland. By selecting CFNI for study, we mean neither to suggest that other organizations have not played important roles (they have), nor that CFNI is the only entity involved in peacemaking efforts worthy of study (it surely is not). Instead, we examined CFNI's efforts because of its prominence in continued peacebuilding initiatives, its broad engagement with a diverse collection of grassroots groups and organizations on all sides of the province's enduring divisions, and its multidimensional peacebuilding programs.

To address our analytic purposes, we first outline how the foundation has defined its overarching role and its more specific responsibilities in peacebuilding, and trace how the character of those aims has shifted over time. For purposes of illustration, we stress particularly the changing nature of the institution's relationships and ties with the European Union, especially its progressively stronger efforts to ensure maximum operating autonomy for its peacebuilding efforts. While we focus on the foundation's ties with the European Union, we recognize that CFNI has had wide-ranging connections with the UK government and many inter-national organizations, local organizations, and foundations besides. We begin by sketching how the foundation's peace-related roles and approach reflect the theoretical claims of leading peacebuilding scholars. We argue that CFNI has adopted a particular process-centered view of peacebuild-ing and of promoting the formation of new narratives of community jus-tice, even as it has sought to redefine its own institutional roles in those processes over the last 25 or so years. Finally, we assess the implications of how foundation leaders are now conceiving the conflict-related tasks of their institution and what those suggest more broadly about the pos-sible roles of NGOs in peacebuilding. In particular, we explore how the CFNI director's use of Foucauldian theoretical tools has yielded a nu-anced approach to peacebuilding based on open and continuous intra-communal engagement with the narratives through which the political imaginaries of war and peace have long been constructed in the prov-ince. CFNI's understanding of peacebuilding as a process rather than an effort of imposing predefined outcomes offers an interesting example of how such endeavors can be reimagined.

Overall, our analysis suggests that CFNI has sought actively to en-courage finding ways and means for antagonists to grapple with alter-nate social imaginaries while simultaneously developing mechanisms by which to secure its own continuing institutional legitimacy and credibil-ity with the populations it serves. It has endeavored to avoid "capture" by the populations with which it works or organizations and groups it supports, while dignifying and engendering the respect of those it aims to assist. The foundation's institutional role in peacebuilding has required persistent attention to the potentially oppressive effects of both conflict-related and peace discourses alike. These narratives have been pressed by authoritative government and supra-governmental actors, have involved the crafting of conflict imaginaries in the communities to be served, and have also taken the guise of funder agendas and priorities.

We argue that CFNI has not sought to demand adoption of a par-ticular social vision by those groups with which it, or its funded interme-diaries, has worked. Its longtime director, who is also a scholar of Michel Foucault and therefore deeply aware of the "thickness" of narratives and contextual determination of meanings, has not taken for granted the ap-parent international consensus on grand rights discourses, but has worked instead to ask groups and organizations from different communities to voice their often divergent understandings of the outcomes they expect from the peace process. In addition, CFNI has invited communities to engage critically with how "war" narratives were formed and how those accounts limited and hardened communal identities. In this way, CFNI has worked to encourage spaces where alternate interpretations of political outcomes may safely be voiced and contested, not a "consensus" that obscures intercommunal differences. The foundation has created opportunities for developing and sustaining a plurality of political perspectives and has consistently sought to ensure that representatives of groups that would otherwise not be countenanced or even acknowledged could be brought to participate in the political process.

CFNI's orientation to conflict resolution assumes that individuals and communities alike can, if permitted ongoing opportunities to reflect actively on the narratives of their enduring enmities and mistrust, singly and with their counterparts find ways and means by which to address the fundamentals of those beliefs and open possibilities to reconstruct them along alternate lines that do not imply enduring conflict. As CFNI staff members told us in our interviews with them, this is both a critical assumption and a bold assertion concerning human cognitive and emotional possibility.[2] Asking individuals and communities to revisit, deconstruct, and build anew the ways in which they are making sense, and have long made sense, of the world implies at least symbolic violence as old values, mores, and norms are challenged and discarded, and strong creative work as new ones are imagined, constructed, shared, and broadly adopted. The processes by which such epistemic-level efforts are sought and sustained are both tortuous and fragile. Little work is more difficult or more challenging than catalyzing possibilities for social change amid enduring hatred and distrust.

CFNI: An Evolving Strategy but Continuing Focus on Catalyzing Potentials for Social Change

The organization that is today the Community Foundation for Northern Ireland was initially established with a grant of £500,000 from the government of the United Kingdom in 1979 as the Northern Ireland Voluntary Trust (NIVT). From the outset, its governing board reflected its service region and included both Protestant and Catholic community leaders. The group's membership was also carefully balanced among male and female members and different social classes. While that composition did not by itself confer social legitimacy or credibility (Brown 2008), it did signal to the parties then in violent conflict that this group would likely prove a partisan of neither side. NIVT was able to match its initial grant by 1984, and the UK government in London provided an additional £500,000 to allow it to continue developing its operational reach and community-centered efforts. By 1990 the trust had established the wherewithal to make grants of £750,000 per year. Dublin native Avila Kilmurray joined the trust as its director in 1994, and in 1995 the European Union selected NIVT to serve as a significant implementing agent for its Special Support Program for Peace and Reconciliation, a role that expanded to include a cross-border development program the following year. In 2000 the trust awarded some £50 million in grants, and in 2001 the EU Northern Ireland Peace Program selected NIVT to continue in a central role in its Peace II initiative for 2001 through 2006. The foundation later agreed to remain involved with the EU effort during its Peace III program from 2007 to 2013, although more selectively.

In 2002 the trust's board formally changed the organization's name to the Community Foundation for Northern Ireland while launching a fund development drive to double its endowment by 2010 to allow the foundation greater discretion in its project selection. This represented a key move by the Community Foundation to secure greater autonomy of action from external international or bilateral donors. UK chancellor of the exchequer Gordon Brown endorsed that campaign in 2003, and Atlantic Philanthropies provided a £3 million challenge grant to spur the effort that same year. As he helped kick off the campaign to match the challenge grant in London, the future prime minister argued,

> Twenty-five years working at the leading edge in Northern Ireland is surely an occasion to celebrate. . . . The Community Foundation is a true survivor of the conflict, and has been a key player in supporting grass-roots peace-building. . . . As an independent grant-maker it has reached people and places that others could not. Closeness to the ground, profound knowledge of need, and highly innovative approach to the engagement of target groups in its decision-making processes have been its trademark. Building civil society, and helping people realise aspirations for a more equitable and positive future remains a challenge for us all and one where the Community Foundation will play its part. It is only in a stable, cohesive, and inclusive society that everyone can contribute to, and benefit from, economic opportunity. The mutual dependence between Government, business and the voluntary and community sectors is clear and I am pleased to endorse the

Community Foundation for Northern Ireland's efforts to build a platform for the future through its fund development campaign. (Community Foundation for Northern Ireland 2007)

In early 2006 the foundation's board of trustees formally announced additional steps to reinforce the foundation's relative operating autonomy. The reason, as Kilmurray wrote in *Alliance Magazine,* was to "place independence before the security offered by government and European Union funding programmes, and to move away from statutory funding in order to cultivate other sources" (Kilmurray 2006). The board considered pursuit of such operating latitude a fundamental prerequisite for the foundation to function as a catalyzer of connections and interaction among local, state, and international stakeholders in peacebuilding efforts. Kilmurray wrote,

> The essential "added value" of independent funding to CFNI is to allow us to innovate and to take calculated risks. The benefit of being a "community" funder is to be close enough to the ground to recognize areas of need long before statutory bodies pick them up, while bringing the expertise and insights of broader networks to the local level. Whether this is sustainable in a small society of one and a half million people remains to be seen. (Kilmurray 2006)

In the same article the director also argued that government and EU funding might actually hinder the foundation's ability to act as a "socially aware funder" committed to justice and sensitive to the ways that traditional patterns of exclusion contributed to ongoing suspicion and conflict among the groups involved:

> The decision to eschew government and EU funding—unless they are adapted to the ethos of the community sector—remains a bold one, but if CFNI is to remain a progressive, socially aware funder, then it must attract investment from organizations that are committed to social justice. By the way, the grants that stirred up the greatest controversy and attracted the greatest volume of hate mail were those to projects in the gay and lesbian community. So even in a conflict-ridden society there is always somebody else to target. (Kilmurray 2006)

This decision to abjure EU funds would, the trustees hoped, enable the foundation to address peacebuilding needs revealed by its grassroots work in communities across Northern Ireland, but which were otherwise often particularly difficult to address. As Kilmurray suggested,

Peacebuilding in a society slowly emerging from conflict was a major challenge. The Political Ex-Prisoner Advisory Committee, formed in December 1995, is made up of representatives from all the Loyalist and Republican paramilitary groups, who come together to consider funding applications for local reintegration and conflict resolution projects, while also informally exchanging views on the ongoing peace process. Important as these meetings are, they have not proved popular with many local politicians and have attracted adverse coverage in the local media. (Kilmurray 2006)

The board indicated its decision was driven in part by a "mature reflection on the fact that neither social justice issues nor effective community action are likely to be progressed through time-limited, micromanaged programmes that at times seem more answerable to the auditor than to the policymaker" (Kilmurray 2006).

Thus, in order to create space to pursue its grassroots community peacebuilding work more creatively and to avoid insistent project-scale accountability demands rooted in short-term evaluative rubrics arising from international donors, the foundation sought to secure more operating and strategic autonomy to make its own choices in the difficult environment in which it was working. CFNI has since continued to work with the European Union, but in a much more selective way (for prisoner reintegration efforts primarily), and has been largely successful in raising funds sufficient to provide it more autonomy in how it proceeds in its philanthropy linked to conflict-related work. Interestingly, however, a significant proportion of that fiscal support comes from beyond Northern Ireland, including from a group established for the purpose in the United States (Kilmurray 2006; Community Foundation for Northern Ireland 2008a).

As the director noted in her *Alliance Magazine* commentary, this strategic choice to rely more heavily on own-source fund-raising was not taken lightly, but was born of frustrations arising from external understandings of peacebuilding imperatives and modes of intervention in communities and conflicts whose sociological contours often did not fit neatly those expectations and ways of operating. CFNI had found that its work in funding grassroots groups and organizations dealt not only with broad fault seams in the society linked to ethnic or sectarian identity but also with a plurality of divides within those differences, and that it inevitably required operating wherewithal to address those complexities if it was to have any hope of securing conditions that might foster a measure of social change (Shirlow and Murtaugh 2004). That outcome was essential if peace was finally to accrue and old habits of enmity rooted in distrust and acculturated hatred were to be broken and reconstructed on different grounds among the parties in conflict. Its experience working with groups on the ground had convinced CFNI staff and leaders that political change in communities occurs only with sustained local-level support for initiatives aimed at promoting a broadly accepted awareness of the divisive effects of conflict identities and at encouraging instead narratives nurturing social justice and inclusion.[3] This community-focused vision is succinctly captured in the Foundation's mission statement: "To drive social change by tackling social exclusion, poverty and social injustice through funding and supporting community-based action and influencing policy development" (Community Foundation for Northern Ireland 2011).

By 2006 the foundation had embarked on what its leaders envisioned to be an ongoing series of efforts to provide opportunities for residents (youth, the middle-aged, and seniors alike) and communities across Northern Ireland to address the assumptions and habits of mind and heart that underpinned the continuing enmities among them. These habituated values and norms were richly textured. CFNI sought to provide a range of occasions for those possessing assumptions to become aware of them, realize their implications, and consider alternatives. Such efforts implied sustained initiatives, adaptive programmatic experimentation, and continuous opportunities for active reflection on organizational strategies. Avoiding failure—in the guise of dismissal from those engaged—in such efforts was a persistent concern. The key to catalyzing potential social change lay in identifying and understanding the basic narratives that underpinned how the conflicting populations were framing their understanding of their daily life experience. In a recent interview Kilmurray suggested that the economic recession beginning in December 2007 had exacerbated political polarization in the province,[4] indicating how malleable emergent imaginaries can be. Unfortunately, the disorder that occurred in summer 2011, above and beyond the usual flaring of tensions associated with the annual parades or marches each year in Belfast and elsewhere in Northern Ireland, suggests the aptness of her observation. We turn next to how CFNI has addressed this central challenge.

Working With the European Community: An Independent Grassroots Player in a Long-Term Multilevel Peace Initiative

Racioppi and See have argued that the design of the EU Special Support Program for Peace and Reconciliation for Northern Ireland reflected strongly the perspectives of two leading thinkers (and practitioners) on peacebuilding, John Paul Lederach and Harold Saunders (Racioppi and See 2007). Following Lederach (1997), the European Union sought to involve organizations and leaders at three tiers of society in its peace initiative. Elected and political leaders would serve as formal and primary negotiators, while mid-range actors, "such as intellectuals, rank-and-file party members, party activists and church members can also serve as brokers between the political elite and the populace at large" (Racioppi and See 2007, 363). Meanwhile, "At the third tier are grassroots activists who are crucial for bottom-up peacebuilding, especially in interface communities, wracked by violence" (Racioppi and See 2007, 363).

Following Saunders, the European Community Northern Ireland initiative stressed the importance of civil society and NGO involvement:

> The concept of the peace process will not be complete until the potential contribution of citizens outside government is recognized and included. It will not be brought into play with full power unless it is seen at the highest levels as operating at both the official and unofficial or public levels. (Saunders 2000, 255)

In sum, the European Community followed the advice of leading thinkers as it devised its initiative and entered into a multilevel peacebuilding effort that sought to address not only economic conditions that might result in violence, but also social and cultural factors that might yield an improved climate for reconciliation. The European Union approached a limited number of NGOs and grassroots-oriented organizations, including CFNI, to serve as what Peace Program leaders dubbed intermediary funding bodies (IFBs), with the goal of ensuring that resources were employed in ways that would maximize the possibilities for including previously marginalized or disaffected groups in peacebuilding efforts. EU initiative leaders looked to the foundation to help address the priority area of conflicts surrounding victims of violence and ex-prisoners especially.

CFNI was most active as an IFB during the first and second phases of the EU Peace Program. Racioppi and See report that the organization was successful in securing a reputation as a neutral arbiter in the efforts with which it was engaged and in encouraging its grantees to consider how their efforts linked not only to conflict amelioration, but also to community development (Racioppi and See 2007). Meanwhile, while the relationship between the foundation and EU Peace Program officials was always cordial, that engagement convinced CFNI leaders that the organization required more autonomy than its IFB role permitted to address the issues its staff saw as critical at the grassroots scale. So, increasingly, while the foundation continued (and continues) formally to embrace a multilevel decentralized cooperative model of peacebuilding intervention, it began to concentrate its funding and efforts firmly on grassroots-scale engagements over which it and its grantees could exercise final discretion concerning program design and implementation. That step, as we previously noted, required developing alternate sources of revenue beyond the UK government and European Community. As we have suggested, the capacity of organizations to remain financially independent by being able to mobilize a multiplicity of supporters while remaining rooted in the communities where they operate are two conditions that appear to be closely linked to peacebuilding success.

Addressing the Problem of Dueling Narratives of Sensemaking for Peace: Are You a State Actor, Loyalist or Republican, Protestant or Catholic?

Many scholars have addressed the notion that community residents frequently share many views and beliefs and that these are as often unreflectively held, because so widely believed. They constitute ways in which populations are together making sense of their worlds. These views and beliefs have political, emotional, and cognitive purport for those who hold them, precisely because they are at play at the epistemic scale and constitute mechanisms by which individuals and groups are making sense of the otherwise bewildering array of relationships, interactions, and factors they confront in their daily lives. For example, the noted Canadian postanalytic philosopher Charles Taylor has addressed the matter of prevailing ways of understanding the world through broadly shared social imaginaries:

> I adopt the term imaginary (i) because my focus is on the way ordinary people "imagine" their social surroundings, and this is often not expressed in theoretical terms, but is carried in images, stories and legends. It is also the case that (ii) theory is often the possession of a small minority, whereas what is interesting in the social imaginary is that it is shared by large groups of people, if not the whole society. Which leads to a third difference; (iii) the social imaginary is that common understanding that makes possible common practices and a widely shared sense of legitimacy. . . . Our social imaginary at any given time

is complex. It incorporates the normal expectations we have of each other, the kind of common understanding that enables us to carry out the kind of collective practices that make up our social life. This incorporates some sense of how we all fit together in carrying out the common practice. Such understanding is both factual and normative; that is, we have a sense of how things usually go but this is interwoven with an idea of how they ought to go, of what missteps would invalidate the practice. (Taylor 2004, 23–24)

The social imaginary is most often implicit, and it confers or takes away legitimacy. Not all in a community need to agree with an imaginary for the construct to prevail as social orthodoxy, but imaginaries typically embody received consensus. For example, many residents of the US South prior to the civil rights movement (1940s–1970s) simply took it as axiomatic that African Americans did not merit the same political rights and social standing as their white counterparts. For all of his puerile rhetoric, in retrospect it seems clear that Alabama governor George Wallace, who served four four-year terms between 1963 and 1987, was simply reflecting that shared imaginary when standing symbolically before the schoolhouse door (Foster Auditorium) at the University of Alabama–Tuscaloosa in June 1963 to bar African American students from entering and desegregating the school. The attitudes and beliefs that Wallace represented went deep for many of his constituents and were themselves the product of long acculturation—to the point that many simply could not conceive of a society differently configured.

By analogy, the same may be said to have been true regarding decades of mistrust, frustration, and victimhood felt deeply on both sides of the conflict in Northern Ireland. Perhaps not surprisingly, profound social change, a complete shift in dominant social imaginaries in the US South, is still incomplete in the United States nearly five decades after Wallace's symbolic act. The same is true in Northern Ireland, which, although it had enjoyed more than 10 years of relative social calm, saw a fresh eruption of violence in summer 2011, suggesting that onetime adherents may fall back to long-lived social imaginaries when economic difficulties or social tensions arise. For CFNI, the key to promoting enduring change in such attitudes is to fund organizations and groups that help those who have adopted them to become aware of them, reflect on them, and understand why they may need to be rethought. This approach often entails a difficult process of revisiting the social narratives that underpin common beliefs and revealing shared interpretations as well as different understandings. These processes typically occasion not a little confusion and emotional angst among those asked to engage in such reflection.

In a recent interview with the authors, Avila Kilmurray indicated that her efforts as a social activist have been influenced by Michel Foucault's work concerning social processes. More specifically she has been inspired by Foucault's thinking concerning narratives and their "thick" and contextual meanings, his exploration of the connections between knowledge and power, and his emphasis on the significance of a variety of administrative procedures and regulations that typically accompany public or governmental implementation of broad normative principles.[5]

In the *Archaeology of Knowledge,* Foucault argued that while the equivalence of sentences can be established based upon their identical logical structures, statements must be understood in the context of the rules that link them to other statements. Thus,

> The identity of a statement is subjected to a second group of conditions and limits: those that are missed are imposed by all the other statements among which it figures, by the domain in which it can be used or applied, by the role and functions it can perform. The affirmation that the earth is round or that a species evolves do not constitute the same statement before and after Copernicus, before and after Darwin; *it is not, for such simple formulations, that the meaning of the words has changed; what changed was the relation of these affirmations to other propositions, their conditions of use and reinvestment, the field of experience, of possible verification of problems to be resolved, to which they can be referred.* (Foucault 1972, 103, emphasis added)

In this view, logical equivalence does not exhaust the possible connotations of statements. While the literal meaning of words may remain constant in different statements, the relations among them may change as the epistemic understandings within which they are situated shift. Foucault argued that statements should be analyzed as part of discursive formations, or in other words, as part of "archives" in which their rules of interaction are established.

For Kilmurray, this Foucauldian insight suggests that the policy advocate must understand how, within an apparent consensus, different communities may nonetheless perceive political processes and priorities differently. While words may remain the same, the epistemic connections of normative statements concerning peace as well as perceptions of the possible practical consequences of their implementation may be very different. To address this concern, CFNI seeks to foster communication processes that attempt to unpack, rather than obscure, such differences. For example, while all sides of a conflict may agree generally on the need to respect human rights, the selection of political processes to achieve that shared goal may be contentious. The same will likely hold for the outcomes of any process selected. Foucault argued that the implications and purport of the exercise of power must be examined when and where they are implemented rather than via abstract analyses of institutional or "legal" forms. With that contention in mind, Kilmurray advocates paying close attention to the practical and administrative level of politics. However, instead of interpreting those processes as "scripts" that cannot be altered and which therefore completely delimit the scope of action available in people's lives (Agamben 1998; Dillon and Read 2009; Edkins, Pin-Fat, and Shapiro 2004; Prozorov 2007), Kilmurray views such dynamics as political opportunities for the stimulation and exercise of political agency.

Kilmurray outlined the different narratives at play in the Northern Ireland conflict in her remarks at the public launch of the Belfast Conflict Resolution Consortium on April 23, 2008, and clearly stated that a key element of the peacebuilding process was to question the perceived solidity of these supposed "truth" constructs among members of the groups involved:

> What I hope to contribute to the discussion this morning are some personal thoughts and reflections on (i) Narrative (the stories that we tell ourselves to make sense of our own circumstances and challenges); (ii) on Codes and Messaging (not 007—or at least not always—but rather how we communicate with both ourselves and others); and (iii) Truth(s), and I deliberately say truths rather than truth, because in a society rooted in conflict and division, what I may see as the truth may be in diametrical opposition from what someone from a different background and community may see as the truth. I then want to conclude my contribution with a couple of strategic and tactical quandaries that we might face in seeking to engage effectively in conflict resolution/ transformation, or even in conflict management. (Kilmurray 2008, 13)

To address her stated concerns, Kilmurray outlined three dominant narratives regarding the nation's conflict and how each evidenced different views of the nation's social reality: that of the state and UK civil service representatives (the United Kingdom's Northern Ireland Office, or NIO), that expressed by Republicans/Nationalists from West Belfast, and that offered by residents of the Unionist/Loyalist greater Shankill community. NIO representatives, Kilmurray argued, offered a view of social reality that sometimes bordered on the surreal, but that was always politically expedient:

> The narrative from the civil service/the state is essentially that they were doing a difficult job, as impartially as possible, trying to bring forward policies to improve conditions and to present the situation as being as normal as possible, despite some clear abnormalities that were unfortunate to say the least. Essentially, Northern Ireland was projected as having genuine social and economic problems; an image problem; and poor relations between the two main communities that resulted in violence. That was the public narrative—it was the fault of local community fears and antagonisms—although [an] NIO interviewee did acknowledge privately that not alone were they talking to everybody behind the scenes all of the time, but also they tried to portray Northern Ireland as basically a normal society having a mid-life crisis, sometimes verged on the absurd. As one of my NIO interviewees said, and I quote—"I mean for years I was writing answers to Parliamentary Questions saying that the RUC (Royal Ulster Constabulary) is normally an unarmed force but in certain circumstances officers are required to carry guns, when you had Inspectors running round with bazookas." (Kilmurray 2008, 12)

Republican/Nationalists, meanwhile,

> tended to be focused on the struggle with Britain and the state—what was striking was the relative lack of attention given to loyalist areas. The narrative held loyalists as dupes; collaborators; political proxies, or if you were a good Marxist, as suffering from "false consciousness"— i.e., dupes with a hint of determinism. As one community activist summed it up—"I just would not believe what I was seeing in front of me, just the viciousness of the system and how powerful they are. And you know, the whole paraphernalia of the tanks, the weapons, the uniforms, all of that there. The structures, the jails, the courts, just the huge monolith that is that power." (Kilmurray 2008, 14)

The director noted that, in this narrative,

> there was a belief that [the Republican Nationalists] were treated as second-class citizens by a Unionist State; they were intimidated into single identity communities by loyalist pogroms; they had to take on the might of the British state, and on top of all this there was the

irritant sectarian attacks by loyalist paramilitaries. In this narrative, the Nationalist/Republican community are on the one hand, victims (both politically and in social and economic terms), but on the other, produced a gallant band of Freedom Fighters, whose role was both to protect a beleaguered community and to assert a national identity and aspiration. (Kilmurray 2008, 14)

Finally, Kilmurray sketched the narrative sustaining the Loyalist/ Unionist social imaginary:

Then, of course, there is the narrative within the Unionist/Loyalist communities which so often, despite expressing abhorrence of Nationalist/Republicanism, was clearly fixated on what they were up to and on what, if any, the relationship was between these communities and the British Government: always expecting the worst. My last little quote comes from the Shankill—"I think in the early days it would have been seen as . . . the more monolithic Republican, Catholic, Nationalist—you know that they were together on this, and that they'd been running a state within a state anyway, and that they were geared up and tooled up; whereas over here we're really needing to build capacity for all our little pockets of stuff that was going on. I think there would have been a perception that we'll be looked after; the Government will—but the realization came that this isn't the case. In fact there would be a perception that the Government are actually buying the peace on the Republican side, that there's much more investment of money going in there in order to get stability on the Republican side, whereas over here we're not as crucially involved." (Kilmurray 2008, 14)

What these otherwise very different stories or visions share is

the perception of victimization, marginalization, being up against the monolithic powerful "other," with the added ingredient of a sense of betrayal. But of course, as Unionist/Loyalists, if your betrayer is also your ultimate protection and home, the focus for attention will invariably be the rebels that are seen as the ultimate cause of all this angst. Of course, what we are talking about here are perceptions—and in some cases perceptions that have been deliberately fuelled by political manipulation—but no less powerful for all that. And it is these very different sets of perceptions—or stories, or narratives—that create our communal commonsense understandings of what is happening to us. Understandings that are particularly honed when we come to discuss sensitive interface issues; or matters of perceived control of territory; and certainly when divisive symbolic issues are on the table. So our conflicting narratives—which, of course, we rarely articulate to each other—are drawn from our very different lived experiences of both the Troubles and the legacy of Unionist rule, are fuelled by mistrust and hurt, while also fuelling further mistrust and fear. (Kilmurray 2008, 14)

Kilmurray concluded her remarks by musing that the conflict had created these dichotomies, which unfortunately continue to fuel the perceptions of thousands and whose allegiants unreflectively code all they hear and see via these filters. Political and social change requires breaking down prevailing representations of the "monolithic powerful 'other.'" Such change is unlikely to occur unless and until those embracing their existing ways of knowing have opportunities to reflect on the implications of those beliefs in light of competing perspectives and to fashion new alternatives to them. In lieu of dwelling, as WIB and the international community in Serbia did, on narratives and identities established during the conflict and attempting to determine what the "truth" was in that regard, Kilmurray and CFNI have instead invited citizens to explore how supposed war "truths" were constructed and to move away from those limited and dichotomized possibilities for understanding communal relations.

As a core aim of its peace-related efforts, CFNI has consistently attempted to provide opportunities for socially disadvantaged groups to voice their concerns and to ensure processes by which such initiatives could be institutionalized. This aspiration implies always being alert and attentive to the exclusion and discrimination that might accompany implementation of otherwise apparently benign agreements on broader principles, even as it suggests energetic continuing efforts to include members of previously marginalized and excluded population groups in peacebuilding processes. In a recent interview with the authors, Kilmurray argued that Northern Ireland politics must ensure space for critical voices, for continuous bottom-up vigilance, so that peace agreement implementation ultimately does not simply sanction a new form of sociopolitical apartheid.[6] For Kilmurray, Foucault's critique of the Enlightenment discourse of rights and his call to examine governmental processes at the scale of administrative institutions, rules, and regulations provides an important reminder to examine continuously the distributive effects of steps taken in the name of peace agreements and to seek ways and means by which to foster the broadest possible political engagement from disparate groups within society.

As part of its efforts to provide opportunities for the otherwise voiceless to be heard, CFNI has sought vigorously to document the testimonies of previously marginalized groups by funding them. In this spirit the foundation has sponsored the filming of histories and perspectives of former prisoners and produced these as videos that have been incorporated into relevant primary and secondary school curricula. Moreover, the foundation has not limited itself to providing opportunities to speak only to the traditional conflicting parties in Northern Ireland. Indeed, it has sought recently to provide a forum for a newly immigrated and marginalized group in Northern Ireland, the Roma people, who find themselves popularly persecuted in the face of currently difficult economic conditions.

CFNI does not limit its activities to promoting reflections on conflict narratives and giving voice to marginalized actors by funding relevant groups mobilized to do so. Indeed, its strategy for peacebuilding includes at least an aspiration for social justice. In a 2010 speech, for example, Kilmurray forcefully argued, "Our ultimate goal must be poverty eradication and not just the amelioration of the difficult circumstances disadvantaged individuals, groups and communities find themselves in" (Kilmurray 2010a). In our 2011 interview with her, Kilmurray suggested that increasing poverty is a serious problem threatening the progress toward the peace thus far achieved in Northern Ireland. Likewise she has contended that monitoring governmental choices may not be enough to secure the progress toward peace attained to date. It is also necessary to promote community mobilization to ensure that poverty does not deepen still further.[7] As she observed in 2010, "It is not enough to monitor, comment and oppose at the macro policy level. We must also organise and respond given the likely increase in poverty and possible curtailment of sources of financial support and service provision" (Kilmurray 2010a).

Kilmurray has also stressed the need to create communication channels between local civil society organizations and other actors in the peace process (Kilmurray 2010a). As the European Union continues to implement major changes in its security policy and various of its member states evidence differences with EU policies, Kilmurray has suggested that civil society should not settle for a least common denominator in peacebuilding, but instead create a network whose relationships could foster organization and social learning at different scales. Such a network could take advantage of the comparative capabilities of its members. Organizations such as CFNI that work with groups and organizations at the grass roots, for example, may know a great deal about peacebuilding in the community, but understand much less about how best to work at the macro level. Similarly, those working at the macro scale often can benefit from (and, as often, require) a reality check concerning the results of policy choices for communities. That "dialogic possibility" implicitly permits space for those at the grass roots to express their needs and concerns and learn from one another (Kilmurray 2010b).

This point is critical. CFNI aims to fund and provide opportunities that seek to promote peace without ordaining it or demanding a particular outcome from participation in such processes. And, as we previously noted, CFNI seeks that result without eliciting "push-back" reactions from those with whom their sponsored organizations are working, whose cherished beliefs are de facto (however artfully) being challenged. The result for grassroots peacebuilders such as CFNI is a very difficult balance between honoring the beliefs of those with whom they are working to choose their own perspectives and providing opportunities for that same population to reflect afresh on the implications of those beliefs and values for the commons or broader society. And this is true even when those perceptions and values may appear absurd, oddly conspiratorial, or worse. The foundation's goal is not to create a single social consensus that it or any other actor articulates, but instead to promote political processes in which extant mechanisms of meaning formation can be brought to the forefront, dissent can be safely voiced, and action can be taken from the bottom up to check proposed "solutions" imposed by any single interest or stakeholder. The danger of conflict and violent reaction when basic beliefs are challenged is real. The upshot of these cross pressures for CFNI has been the adoption of a process-centered view of peacebuilding that seeks to catalyze possibilities for communal engagement, while recognizing a plurality of perspectives and seeking to understand their accompanying underlying assumptions.[8]

The challenges implicit in pursuing a process-focused rather than outcome-oriented approach to social change to secure a more peaceable social order are both political and social. On the political side, such efforts may fall prey to the short-term calculus of many elected leaders whose time frames for action typically include only the next election cycle. It may also succumb to broad public impatience that peace-related initiatives yield tangible benefits for specific groups. Of course, no single methodology or best practice can change hearts and minds or encourage epistemic-scale reflection in the general population in ways certain to result in broadly accepted social outcomes. Instead, this form of action is deeply contextual and therefore as likely to fail as to succeed, and to require repeated efforts to get it right. The issue that this characteristic raises is whether those engaged can find in practice the resources and political support to continue their work and can also develop and sustain the intellectual and emotional toughness and imagination to stay in the fray. Our interviewees indicated that both concerns have been a focus for the foundation since the Belfast Agreement was signed.[9]

On the social side, frames and narratives arise through complex processes of acculturation, and these are not simply the product of processes that may be addressed in peacebuilding-related dialogue and projects. Societies can and do evidence profound structural inequalities that must be rooted out as sources of conflict if intercommunal reconciliation processes are to have a chance to succeed. Aiken has reported marked progress on these factors in Northern Ireland since 1998 (Aiken 2010). Similarly, external conditions, including employment levels and general perceived economic opportunity, may color residents' willingness to search for scapegoats to blame for the situations they are confronting as well as make it less likely that many will take time to engage in peacebuilding-oriented efforts. In an important sense, peacebuilding efforts must negotiate multiple factors if enduring conflicts are to be addressed in a reflective and engaged way. That is, efforts to mitigate conflicts among specific groups must be developed jointly with initiatives to design inclusive, forward-looking policies and development if those populations are to move ahead together on the basis of new social imaginaries.

Conclusion

This chapter has outlined the role of the Community Foundation for Northern Ireland in grassroots community peacebuilding initiatives in Northern Ireland over the last 20 or so years and explored its approach to such processes. During that period the foundation has sought consistently to foster peace by focusing on breaking down intercommunal conflict narratives. CFNI's efforts during this period have gained it local, national, and international respect and accolades even as its leaders have sought self-consciously to secure greater autonomy to react, as its officers elect, to the conflict-related challenges it encounters, while working in the nation's still-divided communities.[10]

To attain this enlarged zone of operating discretion, the foundation has reduced its role and level of interaction with the European Union Program for Peace and Reconciliation even as it has searched actively for alternate sources of revenue for its activities. CFNI has met this challenge partly by fund-raising in Northern Ireland, but also by seeking support from international philanthropies on a matching basis and from individual donors in the United States and the United Kingdom. Given this overarching institutional trajectory, it appears fair to argue the foundation has vigorously sought increased strategic- and operating-level discretion as its understanding of the nature of the challenges implicit in its peace and community-development activities have deepened. Its officers sought greater latitude to act as they perceived necessary, especially to include the previously marginalized in discussions concerning community development and change, in fine-grained ways that recognized the plurality of perspectives at play in the contexts in which CFNI works.

The foundation has embraced a multilevel model of peacebuilding, but it has specialized in working at the grassroots level and has anchored its activities in a perspective of social justice that requires a diverse array of social groups to be permitted a voice in community development and peacebuilding efforts, even when—perhaps especially when—to do so is unpopular or difficult to attain.

Significantly, foundation leaders do not argue that other levels of peacebuilding activity are unimportant, only that CFNI's focus is on grassroots initiatives. Foundation leaders notably distinguish this process-based claim from the imposition or development of any particular view of social justice or order in Northern Ireland's communities, as long as the latter is arrived at via processes that allow all those affected opportunities to voice their concerns or express their perceived needs and interpretations of current and potential narratives of conflict and peace.

The foundation has thus formally encouraged reflection on a diversity of accepted social narratives in its work and has not sought to articulate a single overarching vision of what would constitute a peaceable society. Indeed, its director expressed concern in an interview with the authors that social groups not interpret calls for support of the nation's peace process as a requirement that such efforts not be subjected to ongoing refinement and criticism. In keeping with the foundation's overarching stance to peacebuilding, Kilmurray argued strongly that one might criticize the design, implementation, or outcomes of various peace-related initiatives and not be against peace. However, as the reemergence of some long-lived animosities in the context of the current lingering economic crisis indicates and the EU Northern Ireland Peace Program has also suggested, "intra-communal" reflections on war narratives and identities alone may not be sufficient to address issues that have much more complex root causes.

It also seems clear that CFNI has played an important and relatively autonomous role in peacebuilding at the grassroots level in Northern Ireland since 1998. Of course, it has done little unilaterally and has certainly not claimed to represent the many groups with which it has dealt or which it has funded. Instead, its leaders have sought to ensure that all with a stake in Northern Ireland's future have an opportunity to participate in opportunities aimed at helping its population address the legacy of its conflict-torn past.

In so doing, CFNI appears not to have succumbed to capture by any of the groups it has sought to serve, nor has the Foundation sought to argue that it alone can play any role beyond catalyzing the possibility for what Paolo Freire called "conscientization" or identifying contradictions in experience through dialogue and becoming part of the process of changing the world, with those with whom it works (Freire 2000 [1970]). What occurs thereafter is not within CFNI's province. That represents both a strength and a weakness of the foundation's approach, as it at once honors individual, family, and group capacity to engage with one another on the basis of innovative political imaginaries even as it reveals the clear limits of peacebuilding interventions in societies dedicated to allowing those in conflicting communities agency to address their differences themselves. One corollary of this reality concerns how those working in the foundation must consider the question of time and its significance as they go about their work. On reflection, we have come to think of the foundation as a Janus-like institution, at least as far as time and its peacebuilding efforts are concerned. Even as it seeks to address past events and traumas, CFNI must somehow enable those with whom it works to accept responsibility for looking to the future to produce a new social order for themselves.

The CFNI director sees intra-communal questioning of accepted meaning as a way of revealing the foundational assumptions underpinning the formation of narratives of war and peace, the ambiguities of meaning embedded in peace agreements' principles and norms, the divergent interpretations of such norms by former belligerent communities, and the uneven distributive effects of their implementation. In embracing a Foucauldian view of political engagement, Kilmurray has focused the foundation's efforts on helping the parties in conflict understand and contest supposedly established truths about themselves and their communities and those of other groups. Instead of seeking to outline an ideal model of what Northern Ireland society should be or become, CFNI has chosen to work instead to seek to help those engaged to reveal and challenge the ways in which their widely held conflict narratives are created and sustained, and to be alert to the distributive effects that unconsidered implementation of broader normative claims embedded in peace agreements might entail.

Finally, it also seems clear that CFNI does not possess a magic formula that can automatically result in peace. By promoting intra-community conversations concerning the thickness of alternate social narratives, CFNI has crafted a postmodernist approach to peacebuilding that focuses on nurturing open-ended political processes based on sustained communication and reflection on accepted truths, instead of predefined outcomes or desired preordained solutions. CFNI seeks to encourage critical, alert, and engaged attitudes among the relevant populations with which it works. In this way the foundation has garnered respect, legitimacy, and credibility among the disparate groups it has sought to serve. In short, if CFNI is any indication, NGOs can indeed play vital and important roles in catalyzing potentials for change in peacebuilding processes, keeping in mind the important caveat that those roles are limited by definition. NGOs cannot by themselves overcome structural conditions that could overwhelm them and they cannot substitute for duly constituted governments, but instead they must act through a continuous strategic engagement of different actors, including public ones.

Notes

1. "The Troubles" designates a period of political violence between Protestant Unionists and Catholic Nationalists that lasted formally from the late 1960s until the 1998 "Good Friday" Agreement.

2. CFNI, personal interviews with the authors, May 22–23, 2008; Avila Kilmurray, personal interview, May 22, 2008.

3. Avila Kilmurray, personal interview with the authors, January 2011.

4. Ibid.

5. Ibid.

6. Ibid.

7. Ibid.

8. CFNI staff and executive director, personal interviews with authors, May 2008, January 2011.

9. Ibid.

10. In June 2004 Kilmurray became the first recipient of the Raymond Georis Prize for Innovative Philanthropy in Europe for the foundation's "extraordinary contribution towards alleviating human suffering in the context of

decades of violent political conflict and its considerable record of achievement in building peace in Northern Ireland" (Kilmurray 2004). She was also profiled in then–UK prime minister Gordon Brown's book *Britain's Everyday Heroes* (London: Mainstream Publishing, 2008).

5

Conclusions

And we are here on a darkling plain
Swept with confused alarms of struggle and flight,
Where ignorant armies clash by night.
                              —Matthew Arnold

We have sought in this book to explore how paths for social and political change and engagement in post-conflict (and also, in the case of Partners In Health [PIH], post-disaster) societies can and have been developed in three complex environments in which such efforts have unfolded. Our analysis suggests a number of conclusions. We outline those here, hoping as we do to go beyond sweeping dismissals of NGOs or grand normative aspirations for alternative politics delivered via such organizations, and instead to build on the dynamics of nongovermental organization involvement in peacebuilding. We hope, in short, to move thinking and understanding ahead on the basis of our empirical investigation.

First, our cases illustrate the necessity of actually assessing the implications of enlarged roles for NGOs in international governance if the effects and consequences of their efforts are to be understood not only with consideration to their normative claims or short-term goals but in the context of the broader effects of their engagements. While, in truth, much a priori theorizing has led to the roles that these entities now play, that fact is not sufficient to justify continuing such debates now that these organizations are playing vital parts in post-conflict and post-disaster reconstruction efforts. In our view, the role of NGOs in peacebuilding must instead be explored through analyses of how these organizations are working in situ, in their contexts, as they press to provide services, advocate for change, or mobilize populations.

Relatedly, the experience of Women in Black–Serbia offers a caution concerning making assumptions about how one's peace-related efforts will be received in specific social and political contexts. While few would disagree with WIB's aims to garner visibility and justice for those for whom they advocate (and we are surely in sympathy), the organization's efforts have often been received by targeted governments and groups in ways that made their realization more, not less, difficult to attain. Indeed, perhaps perversely, the NGO's in-principle and absolutist claims often made mobilizing change efforts on behalf of those groups it sought to serve more difficult, in the context of a strong international presence, those addressed so frequently took deep umbrage at the rhetoric and actions aimed at them and translated such claims as another instance of victimizing the Serbian state and people. In the absence of any alternative way for reimagining political community, the organization's insistence on memorializing the atrocities of the war hardened existing political imaginaries and war narratives. We think the advocacy organization's experience underscores the fact that context matters, and interested scholars and policymakers need to learn much more about the ways in which this is so by conducting many more empirical analyses of peace-aimed initiatives, rather than continuing to imagine that macro-level normative claims about justice and human rights are sufficient to the task.

Second, it seems clear that simply turning to NGOs as would-be replacements for ineffective or fragile states is unlikely by itself to secure desired outcomes. Instead, these actions are likely to demand the development of complicated partnerships designed for specific sociopolitical contexts and structured and restructured adaptively as those conditions change, if such partnerships are to prove either durable or appropriate to their avowed or assigned purposes. Analysts need to acknowledge this reality and seek to learn far more about how relevant NGOs and funders are working to manage these complex interactions, what their implications are for ensuring various forms of accountability among all of the entities involved, and what they portend for how funders should structure incentives as well as their own expectations concerning what sorts of results might be attained and how and during what time periods.

As a practical as well as theoretical proposition, it seems clear to us that the increased porosity of state boundaries has not by itself made states irrelevant to post-conflict social reconstruction efforts. NGOs

should not be perceived as a substitute for states, and international donors should not overlook states' continuing roles in improving the long-
term security of their populations. Our analyses of the cases of Haiti and
Northern Ireland suggest that institution building cannot be sustained by
simply redirecting resources from the state to NGOs. Partners In Health's
relative success is in part linked to its decision to work with the Haitian
Health Ministry to provide health services that addressed the needs of
the population it wanted to serve, while contributing to the development of social and institutional capacity. For its part, the Community
Foundation for Northern Ireland (CFNI) has long recognized that it can
catalyze certain sorts of conflict amelioration efforts by funding a variety
of community-based organizations, but it is not equipped alone or in
concert with other INGOs or NGOs to play the roles long undertaken
by the Northern Ireland and UK governments. These must continue to
remain deeply and vigorously engaged in peacebuilding initiatives if social and political change is to occur. NGOs and public players are likely
to enjoy greater success in peacebuilding when working in partnership
with each other and various community stakeholders than either would
working alone or working only with one another.

PIH and CFNI have worked closely with their local governments
to extend or develop relevant capacities to engage in peacebuilding and
service-delivery efforts. Partners In Health has worked assiduously to
share its expertise and to develop relevant Haitian government ability
to deliver health care and produce more sustainable and less conflict-
prone communities. It has done so by insisting on Haitian government
engagement and by creating programs aimed at sharing its own capacities and building companion state competence. Community Foundation
for Northern Ireland, meanwhile, has sought not so much to build government capacities per se, as these were much more present in Northern
Ireland than in Haiti from the start, as to ensure that certain forms of
conflict amelioration and specific groups and geographic areas receive
state attention. CFNI does so by supporting such groups and organizations and their roles in peacebuilding. In addition, in virtually all it has
undertaken and funded, the foundation has sought to engage its many
community partners and the Northern Ireland and UK governments in
its efforts to craft opportunities for relevant population groups to reflect
actively on their assumptions about community and "others" in community. To accomplish their ends, PIH and CFNI have had to develop,
nurture, and manage a complex web of relationships among many actors and to do so without losing sight of their individual missions and

accountability claimants. To the extent that requirements to develop and maintain an array of partnerships with governments and other entities have arisen directly from international official and funder assumptions and demands (and many have), those strictures suggest that those actors should pay much closer attention to the contexts in which they are seeking interventions and to the organizational, programmatic, and leadership imperatives created by their decisions to rely on NGOs as primary actors.

Third, the experience of CFNI and Partners In Health—two otherwise quite different NGOs, at least by mission and subsector of engagement—illustrates the importance of viewing peacebuilding as a long-lived process of engagement and opportunity for adaptation based on active reflection, instead of in preconceived, abstract, and teleological terms. CFNI has sought to avoid the dangers implicit in assuming a predefined vision of what peace should look like for a community enmeshed in long-term enmities; PIH has adopted a needs- and rights-based approach to the provision of health services, and has engaged continuously in reexamining the outcomes of its efforts and adapting its strategies, both for ensuring that its service ends are attained and for guaranteeing its efforts are building relevant governmental and communal capacities for sustainable social change.

Fourth, international normative claims regarding "good governance," "human rights protection," or "peace" are not sufficient to advance social reconciliation or institution building. As the case of WIB suggests, the international strategy to support NGOs that aim to bring about reconciliation by pressing narrow agendas—such as memorializing war crimes and organizing blame along state lines, regardless of how those strategies play in local politics—may simply serve to harden war identities or prevent the formation of an alternative political imaginary not rooted in war.

Moreover, all three cases illustrate how important it is for funders to understand what their would-be reliance on NGOs has wrought: a far more complex environment for the realization of their goals, given the sheer number and variety of actors now enlisted and playing roles in seeking to secure them. This situation requires that international funders and stakeholders interested in developing opportunities for peace in difficult post-conflict environments remain engaged for protracted periods and that they consistently sustain their partners of choice. Chronically underfunded or abandoned NGOs cannot hope to have any possibility of realizing their assigned aims. Similarly, sharply conditional international support to governments is unlikely to build stable institutions. Most importantly, international donors and NGOs alike also need to engage in in-depth analyses of the specific political, economic, and social dynamics at play in the societies under consideration, and avoid as much as possible relying on one-size-fits-all applications of models for peacebuilding. Post-conflict societies are highly politicized spaces. The blurring of spaces of governance in conflict zones among stakeholders from multiple sectors increases the number and diversity of interests and organizations involved and adds to the complexity of political dynamics that their collaboration creates. Social change and capacity building do not occur overnight, and securing them in deeply fraught environments requires sustained experimentation and adaptation. Such processes take time and patience, and they demand prudence.

Fifth, all three cases support a view of peacebuilding as community-focused; forbearing, at least as far as assumptions concerning appropriate "peace ends" are concerned; and humble regarding any actor's capacity to "transform" conflict environments based on abstract aspirations from without. PIH has not only delivered excellent health services, but also sought to build the capacity of Haiti's social and public institutions to address the nation's long-term needs and sustainability, lest it fall back into conflict. CFNI has worked tirelessly with, and funded, community-scale groups to catalyze conversations concerning long-held assumptions of the "other" that might result in changed resident perceptions and behaviors that would reduce social conflict while itself ordaining nothing in that difficult process. Meanwhile, paradoxically, the Women in Black (WIB) case reveals the power and the danger of imagining that peacebuilding can result from imposing broad normative claims, regardless of local politics. As with PIH and CFNI, the WIB experience suggests how strongly significant the political and social context is in shaping the possibilities for would-be peacebuilders.

Last, our three cases point out two interesting dilemmas for forms of international governance that rely on NGOs as ultimate instruments and arbiters of peacebuilding initiatives. All three of our sample NGOs struggled with carving out a measure of discretion to press what they believed were necessary strategies to secure their aims. All three attained some measure of success in securing stable funding streams (most notably PIH and CFNI) apart from INGOs or bilateral agents alone. Nonetheless, these came at some cost in operating latitude and with an accompanying institutional imperative to identify and maintain alternative sources of support over the long term.

Ironically, for the success of peacebuilding efforts, international actors are relying in many cases on the capacity of civil society organizations to develop funding source support apart from the funding they provide so their own claims do not hobble their supposed agents in their efforts to secure peace. This reality suggests another paradox, which we previously noted but wish to underscore here: the international community's turn to NGOs as peacebuilders requires not only that funders monitor and ensure the capacities of their selected actors but also that they do the same for the efforts of those organizations to address local state needs and capacities (by whatever strategy the NGO adopts). While neoliberalism is, we recognize, an ideology, it may nonetheless be prudent for international community leaders to recognize the operational complexities their choices have wrought for peacebuilding efforts. If they are unwilling to change their approach to favor the states they now seek to abandon or avoid, funders should, if they want their extra-governmental initiatives to work, at least be sensitive to the fact that NGOs must develop partnerships and a measure of revenue autonomy, and assist governments in their efforts to develop capacity even as they provide services. Like those they would serve, international leaders may have cause to reflect afresh on their own values and assumptions as those relate to catalyzing peace in post-conflict societies.

References

Agamben, Giorgio. 1998. *Homo sacer: Sovereign power and bare life.* Palo Alto, CA: Stanford University Press.

Aiken, Nevin. 2010. Learning to live together: Transitional justice and intergroup reconciliation in Northern Ireland. *International Journal of Transitional Justice* 4, no. 2: 166–88.

Badie, Bertrand. 2000. *The imported state: The westernization of the political order.* Palo Alto, CA: Stanford University Press.

BBC. 2011. Profile: Ratko Mladic, Bosnian Serb army chief. News Europe Section. May 27. http://www.bbc.co.uk/news/world-europe-13559597.

Beck, Ulrich. 1992 (1986). *Risk society: Towards a new modernity.* London: Sage.

———. 2000. *What is globalization?* Cambridge: Polity Press.

———. 2009. *World at risk.* Cambridge: Polity Press.

Bickerton, Christopher, J. Philippe Cunliffe, and Alexander Gourevitch. 2007. *Politics without sovereignty: A critique of contemporary international relations.* Berkeley: University of California Press.

Biserko, S., and E. Becirevic. 2009. Denial of genocide—On the possibility of normalising relations in the region. http://www.bosniak.org/denial-of-genocide-on-the-possibility-of-normalising-relations-in-the-region/.

B92. 2010a. European Commission delegation chief in Belgrade Vincent Degert supports the initiative for a regional commission for confirming facts about war crimes (REKOM). March 21. http://www.b92.net/eng/news/comments.php?nav_id=65954&version=print.

————. 2010b. Serbs love Kosovo, EU enthusiasm declines. November 17. http://www.b92.net/eng/news/society-article.php?yyyy=2010& mm=11&dd=17&nav_id=70958.

————. 2010c. The Parliament Collegium met today in Belgrade to discuss a new draft declaration, this time condemning crimes committed against Serbs (comments). April 1. http://www.b92.net/eng/news/comments.php?nav_id=66188.

————. 2010d. Activists of several NGOs protested in front of the presidency calling for July 11 to be proclaimed an official day for remembering the Srebrenica genocide (comments). January 11. http://www.b92.net/eng/news/society-article.php?yyyy=2010& mm=01&dd=11&nav_id=64396.

————. 2010e. Declaration represents distancing from crimes. March 31. http://www.b92.net/eng/news/comments.php?nav_id=66187.

Brown, L. David. 2008. *Creating credibility: Legitimacy and accountability for transnational civil society.* Sterling, VA: Kumarian Press.

————, and Vanessa Timmer. 2006. Civil society actors as catalysts for transnational social learning. *Voluntas: International Journal of Voluntary and Nonprofit Organizations* 17, no. 1: 1–16.

Bulatovic, Marko. 2004. Struggling with Yugoslavism: Dilemmas of interwar Serb political thought. In *Ideologies of twentieth-century southeastern Europe,* edited by John Lampe and Mark Mazover, 254–76. Budapest and New York: CEU Press.

Burchell, Graham. 1996. Liberal government and techniques of the self. In *Foucault and political reason,* edited by Andrew Barry, Thomas Osborne, and Nikolas Rose, 19–37. Chicago: University of Chicago Press.

Chandler, David. 2009. Critiquing liberal cosmopolitanism? The limits of the biopolitical approach. *International Political Sociology* 3: 53–70.

Chazan, Naomi. 1992. Africa's democratic challenge. *World Policy Journal* 9, no. 2: 279–307.

Cockaine, James 2009. Winning Haiti's protection competition: Organized crime and peace operations past, present and future. *International Peacekeeping* 16, no. 1: 77–99.

Collier, Paul. 2009. From natural catastrophe to economic security. A report for the Secretary-General of the United Nations. New York: United Nations. www.focal.ca/pdf/haiticollier.pdf.

Community Foundation for Northern Ireland. 2007. Community Foundation for Northern Ireland director profiled in new book by Prime

Minister Gordon Brown. http://www.communityfoundationni.org/download/1/Press Release.pdf.

———. 2008a. Victim empowerment and peacebuilding: Exploring the role of foundations in supporting victim empowerment processes in regions of conflict. May. http://www.foundationsforpeace.org/CFNI_EMPOWER_EXEC_SUM.pdf.

———. 2008b. Victims key to peacebuilding: Victim's Empowerment and Peacebuilding Conference, May 23. http://www.communityfoundationni.org/news/default.asp?ID=39&itemid=75&topicid=6&va=0.

———. 2010. The mission of the Community Foundation of Northern Ireland. http://communityfoundationni.org/opencontent/default.asp?itemid=77&section=LEARN.

———. 2011. Website home page. http://www.communityfoundationni.org/opencontent/default.asp?itemId=1.

DAH Theatre Research Centre. 2010. About us. http://www.dahteatarcentar.com/aboutus.html.

Dean, Mitchell. 1999. Risk, calculable and incalculable. In *Risk and sociocultural theory: New directions and perspectives,* edited by Deborah Lupton, 131–59. Cambridge: Cambridge University Press.

Dillon, Michael, and Julian Reid. 2009. *The liberal way of war: Killing to make life.* New York: Routledge.

Duffield, Mark. 2007. *Development, security and unending war: Governing the world of peoples.* Cambridge: Polity Press.

———, and Nicholas Waddell. 2006. Securing humans in a dangerous world. *International Politics* 43, no. 1: 1–23.

Dugan, Ianthe Jeanne. 2010. Quake has Haiti relying on agricultural roots: Farm Assistance Program, Zanmi Agrikol, expands its sweep to include Port-au-Prince refugees settling in rural areas. *Wall Street Journal,* February 23, http://online.wsj.com/article/SB10001424052748703494404575081744058479892.html.

Economic and Social Council (ECOSOC). 2006. Report of the Economic and Social Council Advisory Report on Haiti, E/2006/69. New York: UN Economic and Social Council. April 11. http://www.un.org/en/ecosoc/docs/report.asp?id=1148.

Edkins, Jenny, Veronique Pin-Fat, and Michael Shapiro (Eds.). 2004. *Sovereign lives: Power in global politics.* New York: Routledge.

Edwards, B., and M. Foley. 2001. Much ado about social capital. *Contemporary Sociology* 30, no. 3: 227–30.

Farmer, Paul. 2001. *Infections and inequalities: The modern plagues.* Berkeley: University of California Press.

———. 2011. *Haiti after the earthquake.* New York: PublicAffairs Books.

Ferrara, Cecilia. 2010. Serbia: Towards a regional truth on war crimes. *Osservatorio Balcani e Caucaso.* January 12. http://www.balcanicaucaso.org/eng/Regions-and-countries/Serbia/Serbia-towards-a-regional-truth-on-war-crimes.

Foucault, Michel. 1972. *The archaeology of knowledge.* New York: Pantheon Books.

———. 1973. *The order of things.* New York: Vintage Books.

Freire, Paolo. 2000 (1970). *Pedagogy of the oppressed.* New York: Continuum.

Hallward, Peter. 2007. *Damming the flood: Haiti, Aristide, and the politics of containment.* London: Verso Books.

Harati, Donna. 2009. The Advocacy Project. http://advocacynet.org/wordpress-mu/dharati/.

Hardt, Michael, and Antonio Negri. 2000. *Empire.* Cambridge, MA: Harvard University Press

Harvey, David. 2005. *A brief history of neoliberalism.* Oxford: Oxford University Press.

Hatzopoulos, Pavlos. 2008. *The Balkans beyond nationalism and identity: International relations and ideology.* London: I.B. Tauris.

International Crisis Group. 2009. *Haiti: Stability at risk.* Latin America and Caribbean Briefing Report no. 19. Port-au-Prince/Brussels, March 3.

———. 2010. *Haiti: Stabilization and reconstruction after the quake.* Latin and Caribbean Report no. 32, March 31.

Kaldor, Mary. 2003. *Global civil society: An answer to war.* Cambridge: Polity Press.

Kennedy, David. 2004. Reassessing international humanitarianism: The dark sides. Speech presented at the Allen Hope Southey Memorial Lecture, University of Melbourne Law School, June 8. http://www.law.harvard.edu/faculty/dkennedy/speeches/.

Kilmurray, Avila. 2004. Interview: Avila Kilmurray. *Alliance Magazine.* August. http://www.alliancemagazine.org/node/2037.

———. 2006. Community Foundation for Northern Ireland: Peacebuilding and participation. *Alliance Magazine.* March. http://www.alliance magazine.org/en/content/community-foundation-northern-ireland-peacebuilding-and-participation.

————. 2008. Keynote address, in conference report. From Confrontation to Co-Operation: Grassroots Conflict Resolution. Belfast Conflict Resolution Consortium, April 23. http://www.bcrc.eu/ publications.php, 12–15.

————. 2010a. Crisis Speech at the Making the Best of a Crisis event in Belfast, September 27. http://www.communityfoundationni.org/ filestore/default.asp?itemId=79.

————. 2010b. Avila Kilmurray on foundations' contribution to peace and security. EuroFoundation Centre, June 1. http://www.youtube .com/watch?v=cNhohl2ey2Q.

Lawless, Robert. 1992. *Haiti's bad press*. Rochester, VT: Schenkman.

Lederach, John Paul. 1997. *Building peace: Sustainable reconciliation in divided societies*. Washington DC: United States Institute of Peace Press.

Lipschutz, R., and J. Rowe. 2005. *Globalization, governmentality and global politics: Regulation for the rest of us?* London: Routledge.

Marchetti, Raffaele, and Nathalie Tocci. 2009. Conflict society: Understanding the role of civil society in conflict. *Global Change, Peace and Security* 21, no. 2: 201–17.

————. (Eds.). 2011. *Conflict society and peacebuilding: Comparative perspectives*. London and New York: Routledge.

OECD. 2008. *Concepts and dilemmas of state building in fragile situations*. Paris. www.oecd.org/dataoecd/61/45/38368714.pdf.

Partners In Health. 2010a. Director's statement. http://PIH.org/who/ director.html.

————. 2010b. June PIH e-bulletin. http://www.pih.org/pages/pih-e-bulletin-2010-06.

————. 2010c. Partners In Health home page. www.PIH.org.

————. 2010d. The PIH Model of Care. http://www.PIH.org/what/ PIHmodel.html.

————. 2010e. Who we are. http://www.PIH.org/who/vision.html.

————. 2010f. Haiti/Zanmi Lasante. http://www.pih.org/pages/haiti.

————. 2011g. PIH Co-founder Paul Farmer testifies at Senate Foreign Relations Committee. http://www.pih.org/haiti/news-entry/ pih-co-founder-paul-farmer-testifies-at-senate-foreign-relations-committee/.

Prozorov, Sergei. 2007. *Foucault, freedom, and sovereignty*. Burlington, VT: Ashgate Publishing.

Racioppi, Linda, and Katherine O'Sullivan See. 2007. Grassroots peace-building and third-party intervention: The European Union's special support programme for peace and reconciliation in Northern Ireland. *Peace and Change* 32, no. 3: 361–89.

Rhodes, R.A.W. 1996. The new governance: Governing without government. *Political Studies* 44, no. 4: 652–67.

Richard, B., and C. Mcloughin. 2010. Engagement with non-state service providers in fragile states: Reconciling state-building and service delivery. *Development Policy Review* 28, no. 2: 131–54.

Richmond, Oliver. 2009. Becoming liberal, unbecoming liberalism: Liberal-local hybridity via the everyday as a response to the paradoxes of liberal peacebuilding. *Journal of Intervention and State-building* 3, no. 3: 324–44.

———. 2005. *The transformation of peace.* Basingstoke, UK: Palgrave McMillan.

———, and Henry Carey. 2005. *Subcontracting peace: The challenge of NGOs peacebuilding.* Burlington, UK: Ashgate Publishing.

Rose, Nikolas. 1996. Governing "advanced" liberal democracies. In *Foucault and political reason,* edited by Andrew Barry, Thomas Osborne, and Nikolas Rose, 37–64. Chicago: University of Chicago Press.

Rose, Pauline. 2007. *Supporting non-state providers in basic education service delivery.* Report for DFID Policy Division, Consortium for Research on Educational Access, Transition and Equity (CREATE), Sussex University, June.

———. 2009. NGO provision of basic education: Alternative or complementary service delivery to support access to the excluded? *Compare* 39, no. 2: 219–33.

Sansom, K. 2006. Government engagement with non-state providers of water and sanitation services. *Public Administration and Development* 26, no. 3: 207–17.

Saunders, Harold. 2000. Interactive conflict resolution: A view for policy makers on making and building peace. In *International conflict resolution after the Cold War,* edited by Paul Stern and Daniel Druckman, 251–93. Washington DC: National Academies Press.

Schmitter, Philippe C. (with the assistance of Nicholas Guilhot and Imco Brower). 1997. *Defining, explaining and using the concept of "Governance."* European University Institute and Stanford University. Unpublished working paper.

Schwartz, Timothy. 2008. *Travesty in Haiti: A true account of Christian missions, orphanages, fraud, food aid, and drug trafficking.* Charleston, SC: BookSurge Publishing.

Shirlow, Peter, and Brendan Murtaugh. 2004. Capacity building, representation and intracommunity conflict. *Urban Studies* 41, no. 1: 57–70.

———. 2006. *Belfast: Segregation, violence and the city.* London: Pluto Press.

Simons, Marlise. 2011. Mladic arrives in the Hague. Europe Section, May 31. http://www.nytimes.com/2011/06/01/world/europe/01serbia .html?scp=1&sq=Ratko%20Mladic%20extradited&st=cse.

Sörensen, Jens. 2010. Aid policy, civil society and ethnic polarisation. In *Challenging the aid paradigm: Western currents and Asian alternatives,* edited by Jens Sörensen, 78–105. London: Palgrave Macmillan.

Taylor, Charles. 2004. *Modern social imaginaries.* Durham, NC: Duke University Press.

Thomas, Carolyne. 2001. Global governance, development and human security: Exploring the links. *Third World Quarterly* 22, no. 2: 159–75.

Tickner, Anne. 2001. *Gendering world politics: Issues and approaches in the post–Cold War era.* New York: Columbia University Press.

United Nations. 1999. *Report of the Secretary-General pursuant to General Assembly Resolution 53/35. The Fall of Srebrenica.* A/54/ 549. November 15.

United Nations Department of Peacekeeping Operations. 2008. *United Nations peacekeeping operations principles and guidelines.* New York: United Nations.

United Nations Development Program. 1994. Human Development Report. New York: United Nations.

———. 1997. *Governance for sustainable growth and equity.* Report of International Conference, New York, July 28–30, 1997. New York: United Nations.

United Nations General Assembly. 1998. *Support by the United Nations system of the efforts of governments to promote and consolidate new or restored democracies.* A/53/554. New York: United Nations.

———. 2000. *United Nations International Support Mission in Haiti.* A/55/618, November 9. New York: United Nations.

———. 2004. *A more secure world: Our shared responsibility.* Report of the High-Level Panel on Threats, Challenges and Change. A/59/ 565. New York: United Nations.

———. 2005. *In larger freedom: Towards development, security and human rights for all.* A/59/2005. New York: United Nations.

United Nations Security Council. 2000. Resolution 1325. http://www .un.org/events/res_1325e.pdf.

Van Slyke, D. 2007. Agents or stewards: Using theory to understand the government-nonprofit social service contracting relationship. *Journal of Public Administration Research and Theory* 17, no. 2: 157–87.

Vaux, T., and E. Wisman. 2005. *Service delivery in countries emerging from conflict.* Final report for DFID. Bradford, UK: University of Bradford, Centre for International Co-operation and Security.

Vuskovic, L., and Z. Trifunovic. 2008. *Women's side of war.* Belgrade: Women in Black–Belgrade.

Women in Black. 2006. Published proceedings from the Women in Black sponsored conference, Security in Europe for whom? Which Europe do we want? http://www.zeneucrnom.org/index.php?option=com_content&task=view&lang=en&id=246.

———. 2010a. Women in Black website. www.zeneucrnom.org/.

———. 2010b. Women's Feminist, Antimilitarist Peace Organization. http://www.zeneucrnom.org/index.php?option=com_content&task=blogcategory&id=2&Itemid=4&lang=en.

World Bank. 1992. *Governance and development.* Washington DC: World Bank.

Zajovic, S., M. Perkovic, and M. Urosevic (Eds.). 2007. *Women for peace.* Belgrade: Women in Black–Belgrade.

Zanotti, Laura. 2005. Governmentalizing the post–Cold War international regime: The United Nations debate on democratization and good governance in the 1990s. *Alternatives: Local, Global, Political* 30, no. 4: 461–87.

———. 2008. Imagining democracy, building unsustainable institutions: The UN Peacekeeping Operation in Haiti. *Security Dialogue* 39, no. 5: 539–61.

———. 2010. Cacophonies of aid, failed state building and NGOs in Haiti: Setting the stage for disaster, envisioning the future. *Third World Quarterly* 31, no. 5: 755–71.

About the Authors

Max Stephenson Jr. is Professor of Public and International Affairs and Director of the Institute for Policy and Governance at Virginia Tech. He has published widely on civil society and governance concerns. His current research and teaching interests include civil society studies, NGOs and international development, peacebuilding, humanitarian relief, environmental justice, and community change processes. His work has been published in many journals and recently, he coedited *Building Walls and Making Borders: Social Imaginaries and the Challenge of Alterity* (Ashgate Publishers, 2013).

Laura Zanotti is an associate professor of political science at Virginia Tech. Her research and teaching include critical political theory as well as international organizations, UN peacekeeping, democratization, and the role of NGOs in post-conflict governance. She has recently published a new book, entitled *Governing Disorder: United Nations Peace Operations, International Security, and Democratization in the Post–Cold War Era* (Penn State University Press, 2011). Zanotti has published in many peer reviewed journals, including *Alternatives, International Peacekeeping, The Journal of International Relations and Development, Security Dialogue, Third World Quarterly,* and *Global Policy* and has contributed chapters to several edited books. Prior to joining Virginia Tech, Zanotti worked for about ten years at the United Nations where she served in administration and as a political officer for Peacekeeping Operations. She has spent several years in the field in Haiti and in the Balkans. Between 2001 and 2003 she performed as the Deputy to the Head of the United Nations Liaison Office in Zagreb, Croatia.

Index

Also available from Kumarian Press

Creating a Better World: Interpreting Global Civil Society
Edited by Rupert Taylor

"In a world riven by global conflict and struggling to build effective global governance, the crucial missing ingredient is global civil society. Rupert Taylor and his colleagues here provide a guide for how recent protests inform efforts to build a global civil society on which our very survival may yet depend."

—*Anthony W. Marx,*
Professor of Political Science and President, Amherst College

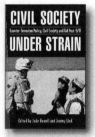

Civil Society Under Strain:
Counter-Terrorism Policy, Civil Society and Aid Post-9/11
Edited by Jude Howell and Jeremy Lind

"Presents a compelling case for the need to understand the connections between the global security agenda and national and local politics. The summative message of this critically important collection is that across different country contexts, the so-called 'war on terror' has ricocheted through civil society organizations in ways that are actually and potentially damaging to state-society relations and to international aid and development."

—*Professor Jo Beall,*
Deputy Vice Chancellor, University of Cape Town

Building Peace: Practical Reflections From the Field
Edited by Craig Zelizer and Robert A. Rubinstein

"This volume provides an enlightening, encouraging, and fascinating set of reports about effective peacebuilding endeavors. These accounts and assessments were written by persons directly engaged in each undertaking and yield valuable lessons. Certainly, these highly diverse actions deserve widespread attention and frequent emulation."

—*Louis Kriesberg,* Professor Emeritus of Sociology,
Maxwell Professor Emeritus of Social Conflict Studies,
Syracuse University

Visit Kumarian Press at **www.kpbooks.com** or call **toll-free** 800.232.0223 for a complete catalog.

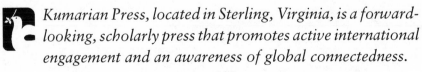

Kumarian Press, located in Sterling, Virginia, is a forward-looking, scholarly press that promotes active international engagement and an awareness of global connectedness.